01109

D1405677

MODERN WORLD NATIONS

R

Rwanda

Joseph R. Oppong

Series Editor
Charles F. Gritzner
South Dakota State University

CHELSEA HOUSE PUBLISHERS
An imprint of Infobase Publishing

Frontispiece: Flag of Rwanda

Cover: A boy uses a can filled with rocks to chase birds from a wheat field, Ruhengeri, Rwanda.

Rwanda

Copyright © 2008 by Infobase Publishing

Chelsea House
An imprint of Infobase Publishing
132 West 31st Street
New York NY 10001

Library of Congress Cataloging-in-Publication Data

Oppong, Joseph R.
  Rwanda / Joseph R. Oppong.
    p. cm. — (Modern world nations)
  Includes bibliographical references and index.
  ISBN 978-0-7910-9669-7 (hardcover)
  1. Rwanda—Juvenile literature. I. Title. II. Series.

  DT450.14.O67 2008
  967.571—dc22   2007040323

Chelsea House books are available at special discounts when purchased in bulk quantities for businesses, associations, institutions, or sales promotions. Please call our Special Sales Department in New York at (212) 967-8800 or (800) 322-8755.

You can find Chelsea House on the World Wide Web at http://www.chelseahouse.com

Series design by Takeshi Takahashi

Cover design by Jooyoung An

Printed in the United States of America

Bang NMSG 10 9 8 7 6 5 4 3 2 1

This book is printed on acid-free paper.

All links and Web addresses were checked and verified to be correct at the time of publication. Because of the dynamic nature of the Web, some addresses and links may have changed since publication and may no longer be valid.

Table of Contents

MODERN WORLD NATIONS

Rwanda

1

Introducing Rwanda

Rwanda! The very name evokes troubling images of unparalleled violence and senseless human atrocities, including widespread genocide. The country is best known as the site of what may have been the world's most grotesque recent example of ethnic-based conflict. In 1994, approximately one million people were killed in 100 days, and millions more fled the country. As this occurred, the world looked on passively, watching on TV the daily carnage of human butchery often inflicted by machetes and other primitive weapons. The sad but true story is captured in the film *Hotel Rwanda.* These images of violence, hunger, starvation, and rape, all stemming from ethnic differences, have led some to call Rwanda "the land of genocide." But there is more to Rwanda than ethnic-based violence.

Rwanda is tiny, about the size of Maryland, but it has many names. Due to its mostly hilly terrain, it has been called the "land of a

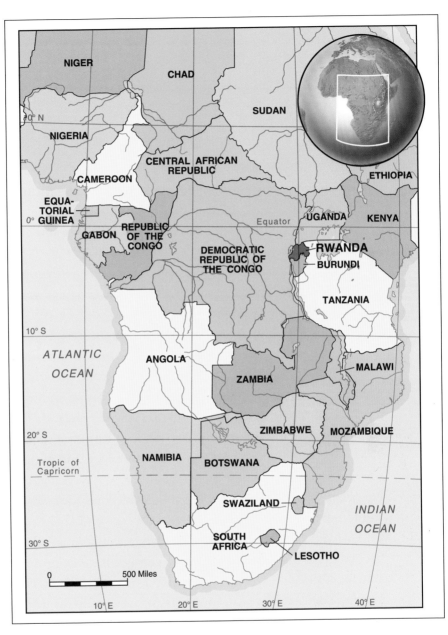

The Republic of Rwanda is located in the Great Lakes region of east-central Africa. With nearly 10 million citizens in an area about the size of Maryland (10,170 square miles, or 26,338 square kilometers), it is the most densely populated country in Africa. It is bordered by Uganda, Burundi, the Democratic Republic of the Congo, and Tanzania.

thousand hills." It also is the home to many gorillas and the site of naturalist Dian Fossey's amazing work to save this endangered species. Her efforts were captured in the movie *Gorillas in the Mist*, which is why some people call the country the "land of Gorillas in the Mist." Early European travelers admired Rwanda's striking natural beauty. They called the country the "Pearl of Africa." Others were awed by the country's mountainous and terraced landscapes and dubbed it the "Switzerland of Africa." Native Rwandans have an even more profound name—*Rwanda Nziza*, or simply, beautiful Rwanda. These many names capture different aspects of the incredible variety of natural beauty that is called Rwanda.

Rwanda is a landlocked country. Located in the heart of East Africa, the country is exactly midway between Cape Town in South Africa and Cairo in Egypt. It shares borders with the Democratic Republic of the Congo (DRC) to the west, Uganda to the north, Tanzania to the east, and Burundi to the south. From the capital, Kigali, the nearest port from the Indian Ocean is at least 1,000 miles (1,600 kilometers) away, and from the Atlantic Ocean at least 1,300 miles (2,200 kilometers). This location makes foreign trade difficult due to extra transportation costs. Imports are relatively more expensive and exports are less competitive on the global market.

Most of what Americans may know about Rwanda no doubt relates to the recent history of violence and bloodshed. Following the 1994 genocide—the deliberate attempt of ethnic groups to kill one another—Rwanda engaged the DRC in 1996 in what ultimately became known as Africa's World War. That war involved seven African countries and resulted in the deaths of an estimated 3 million Congolese, most of whom died from hunger and disease. In addition, millions more were internally displaced in the DRC, or fled the country as refugees. Even now, Rwanda and Uganda continue to have some unresolved conflicts that result in occasional outbreaks of violence.

Why does such a beautiful country have such a violent history? Does the physical environment have anything to do with it? What role did the historical activities of European colonists play in the 1994 crisis? After such a devastating crisis, what are the prospects for peace and recovery for Rwanda? These are some of the many questions we will try to answer as we explore the intriguing geography and mystique of Rwanda and its people.

This book presents a geographer's view of Rwanda. It begins with an assessment of the country's physical geography. We will probe ways in which population pressures and environmental resource use may have contributed to the Rwandan genocide of 1994. Also, we will attempt to understand why Rwanda's location contributes to frequent shake-ups, both natural and human. The country experiences frequent earthquakes. It also experiences frequent conflicts with neighboring countries such as the DRC, Burundi, and Uganda. We will also examine the role mineral wealth in the DRC has played in creating conflict between the two countries. In this context, you will better understand how abundant natural wealth has come to be known as a "resource curse" in this troubled part of the world.

Rwanda provides an exciting opportunity to explore many fascinating themes in physical, human, and historical geography. Did you know, for example, that uncontrolled conflict in one country affects neighboring countries? It is just like a house fire. Uncontrolled, it can spread to neighboring homes and continue the devastation. Political geographers have a fascinating theory to explain this. It is called the *domino theory*. This theory states that uncontrolled conflict in one country triggers conflicts in neighboring countries. Think about other countries where this holds true. The domino theory will be applied to explain the political instability in equatorial African countries including Burundi, Rwanda, and the DRC. It will also

Numbering at only about 700, mountain gorillas face high risk of extinction due to habitat loss, poaching, human disease, and war. They make their home in the dense forests spanning the border between Uganda, Rwanda, and eastern Congo and draw thousands of tourists each year.

help to illustrate how conflict forces populations to migrate, thereby creating refugees and displaced families.

The dynamic relationship between humans and their natural environment—especially population growth and land resource use—are vividly illustrated in Rwanda. By 1984, virtually all available agricultural land in Rwanda was under cultivation. But the population continued to grow at 3 percent annually. With no new lands to cultivate, Rwandans resorted to more intensive cultivation of the land, including shorter fallow periods and rotation times. The number of cattle per acre of land increased significantly as well. All these factors led to more rapid soil depletion and exhaustion and a sharp increase in tensions and conflicts over land ownership.

Rwanda is located in the transitional zone between the forest ecosystems of the Congo basin to the west and the Great Rift Valley to the east. This position has contributed to the country's extremely rich biological diversity. The natural wildlife includes hippopotamuses, elephants, buffalo, cheetahs, lions, zebras, leopards, jackals, hyenas, wild boar, antelopes, crocodiles, and an incredible variety of birds. To crown all this, Rwanda is home to the last remaining population of wild mountain gorillas. This range of primate species is unusual in its number and diversity.

Besides the rich natural environment, the ways in which people have culturally adapted to their surroundings are equally amazing. For example, in the challenging hilly environment extending from about 5,000 to 7,000 feet (1,500 to 2,100 meters) in elevation, Rwandans have constructed beautiful terraces. On what once were slopes too steep to cultivate, tea and coffee plantations now thrive on the human-made terraced landscape.

There are many other amazing facts about the country. For example, in 2007, Rwanda had more women in parliamentary positions than any other country in the world. It has not always been so, however. In fact, prior to the genocide, women were considered minors in Rwanda and could not qualify for credit without the approval of their husbands. Today things are much different. Women have a major role in society, but electing a female as president still appears to be a distant and almost unimaginable dream.

Despite all its difficulties, Rwanda is on track to become the "Silicon Valley of East Africa." Thanks to Google, the Bill Gates Foundation, and other philanthropic organizations, Rwanda is determined to become the information technology giant of

East Africa. Already most villages are connected through telnet centers, and every primary school has computers. This is very unusual in an African country.

In addition, Rwanda is developing its own film industry. Affectionately called "Hillywood," the name reflects both the mountainous beauty of Rwanda itself and the aspirations of its young filmmakers. The low-cost films employ Rwandan actors and actresses, are made by Rwandan directors and producers, are filmed in Rwanda, and use the local language, Kinyarwanda. So far, the themes have focused on Rwanda-related stories, including the genocide. Rwanda's young people are exceptionally creative, and the film industry appears to be on the rise. In fact, the future of the country's film industry holds great promise for the future.

As we explore Rwanda, we will experience both its sad history and exciting future. We will meet *kadogo*, child soldiers who were forced to fight in the conflicts. We will meet other children orphaned by genocide or HIV/AIDS. We will visit with Paul Kagame, the brave and bold president of this troubled country. He has the task of charting new ground for post-genocide economic recovery, while personally facing accusations of crimes against humanity stemming from the 1994 crisis.

In summary, Rwanda is a tiny, beautiful, and troubled land. It has limited natural resources and faces a severe land shortage. But it has a bright future based on information technology. Let us go and visit the country and learn the secrets of Rwanda's resilience and enjoy its night life. Welcome to beautiful Rwanda!

CHAPTER

2

Physical Landscapes

With a total land area of only 10,170 square miles (26,338 square kilometers), Rwanda is a rather tiny country tucked away in central East Africa. It is about the same size as the state of Maryland. At its extremes, Rwanda measures 154 miles (248 kilometers) from northeast to southwest, and 103 miles (166 kilometers) from southeast to northwest. It is located just two to three degrees south of the equator, placing the country squarely within Earth's tropical zone. In this chapter, you will learn not only about Rwanda's natural environmental conditions. You also will better understand the close relationship that exists between nature and the people who depend upon Earth and its resources for their survival.

A RUGGED TERRAIN

Most of Rwanda is hilly, a plateau surface, or mountainous, rising at least 4,000 feet (1,220 meters) above sea level. Elevation is lowest in the south and east and highest in the north and west. In the north-west are the Virunga Mountains. This volcanic range stretches for about 50 miles (80 kilometers) along the border with the Democratic Republic of the Congo (DRC) and Uganda. In the central part of the country, a plateau terrain generally ranges between 4,950 to 6,600 feet (1,500–2,000 meters) above sea level. The western part of this plateau, at an average elevation of almost 9,000 feet (2,750 meters) is a mountain range that serves as the divide between Africa's two most important rivers—the Nile and the Congo. The Nile is Africa's longest river, and the Congo is the second longest and largest by far in terms of volume. On the western slopes of this ridgeline, the land slopes abruptly toward Lake Kivu and the Ruzizi River Valley. These features form Rwanda's western boundary with the DRC. The eastern slopes are more moderate, with rolling hills and descending elevations. Gradually, the uplands give way to the plains, swamps, and lakes of the eastern border region. The Kagera River, which forms much of Rwanda's eastern border, flows into Lake Victoria.

The Virunga volcanic range covers the entire area north and east of Lake Kivu, where Uganda, Rwanda, and the DRC meet. Rwanda's highest peak, snowcapped Mount Karisimbi (14,826 feet, or 4,519 meters), is a part of this system. Virunga, which means "volcanoes," includes eight volcanic peaks, some of which are active and others of which remain dormant. Two very active volcanoes, Nyirangongo and Nyamlagira, erupted several times in the 1980s and 1990s and again in 2002 and 2006. The most recent eruptions caused massive destruction in Goma, a city of about 160,000 located just across the border in the DRC. The steep slopes of the Virunga Mountains are heavily forested and provide one of the few remaining habitats for the mountain gorilla. The entire area is protected within the Parc National des Volcans.

Wait a minute. Did you say *snowcapped* mountains in Africa? Yes, snow in Africa; in fact, snow and even glaciers are just a short distance from the equator. Temperatures generally

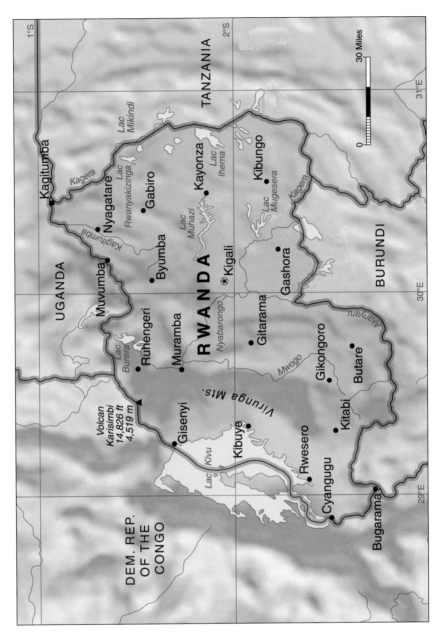

Despite being only two degrees south of the equator, Rwanda enjoys a temperate climate because of its altitude. This small, fertile country of hilly terrain is also called "Land of a Thousand Hills." The Virunga Mountains, a range that consists of eight volcanoes, includes Volcan Karisimbi, Rwanda's highest peak (14,787 feet, or 4,507 meters). The mountains are home to the endangered mountain gorilla.

decrease with increased elevation. Geographers call this the environmental lapse rate. The average environmental lapse rate is a decrease of 3.6°F per 1,000 feet increase in elevation (6.5°C/1,000 meters). Thus, at the peak of Mount Karisimbi, one might expect the temperature to be about 36°F (21°C) lower than in the central plateau region of Rwanda, where the average elevation is between 4,950 and 6,600 feet (1,500–2,000 meters).

AFRICA'S GREAT RIFT VALLEY

Rwanda lies on the western extension of East Africa's Great Rift Valley, a huge 6,000-mile long (9,656-kilometer) crack in Earth's crust. This spectacular landform feature stretches from Lebanon in the north to Mozambique in the south. It was produced by tectonic (geologic faulting) activity. The main Rift Valley runs from the Jordan River Valley and the Dead Sea southward to form the Red Sea. Then it crosses Ethiopia, Kenya, Tanzania, and Malawi to disappear in the lower Zambezi River Valley in Mozambique. The western branch runs along the eastern border of Rwanda and the DRC.

Geologists say this part of Africa is being pulled apart and will become a new sea in the distant future. Tectonic forces in Earth's crust caused huge chunks of the crust to sink between parallel fault lines. As this occurred, the action forced molten rock upward, where it reached the surface as volcanic eruptions. The many active volcanoes and numerous boiling hot springs indicate that the geologic activity is ongoing. Eventually, as the rift deepens and widens, surrounding waters will rush in to create a new gulf, or sea. And the land that is now Somalia will break away from the African mainland to become a large island.

The chain of lakes in East Africa that includes Lakes Kivu, Tanganyika, Edward, Albert, Turkana, and Nyasa, are part of this system. Most lakes that occupy the Great Rift Valley are long and narrow. They also are deep. Lake Tanganyika stretches from northern Zambia in the south to Burundi in the north; it forms the border between the DRC and Tanganyika and is the world's second deepest freshwater body. Its maximum depth is 4,823 feet (1,470 meters), second only to Siberia's Lake Baikal. Let us look more closely at one of these East African Great Lakes: Lake Kivu.

Lake Kivu

At 4,790 feet (1,460 meters) above sea level, Lake Kivu is Africa's highest lake. The water body drains into Lake Tanganyika through the Ruzizi River at a very steep angle due to the sharp elevation difference. Lake Kivu is unique. According to scientists, the geological history of Lake Kivu indicates that approximately every thousand years a startling and potentially devastating event occurs. Its water suddenly overturns, when a lake saturated with carbon dioxide suddenly erupts or explodes. A lake overturn, or limnic eruption, is a rare natural disaster. This turbulent action results in the death of all creatures living in the lake. It also causes widespread devastation to plant and animal life in the surrounding area. Kivu is one of the very few lakes in the world that contains such a large amount of carbon dioxide at its lower levels. As a result, this bottom water could again overturn at any time. Such an event is rare, but it does happen, and often with destructive results. In the event of an overturn, huge amounts of carbon dioxide would be released, and this would suffocate any living creatures in the immediate vicinity. Moreover, massive amounts of methane are trapped beneath the lake's water. Were this volatile gas to be released, it could cause major explosions.

Such an event actually happened in Cameroon's Lake Nyos in 1986. Like Lake Kivu, Lake Nyos has huge amounts of methane and carbon dioxide trapped underneath the water due to ongoing tectonic activity. On August 21, 1986, a methane gas explosion threw a column of water and an enormous quantity of carbon dioxide high into the air. The carbon dioxide flowed into the surrounding valleys and killed all forms of life within an 18-mile (30-kilometer) radius of the lake. At least 1,800 people died in this natural catastrophe. The toll on fish and other wildlife was huge. If this happened in Rwanda, the devastation would be much worse. Not only is the area more densely populated, but the methane in Lake Kivu is estimated to be more than 1000 times greater than it was in Lake Nyos.

This does not have to happen. Efforts are now underway to tap the methane at the bottom of the lake as an important source of energy. Lake Kivu contains an estimated 85 billion cubic yards (65 billion cubic meters) of methane. If tapped, it would provide Rwanda with an almost inexhaustible source of energy. And there would be an endless supply of gas, because Lake Kivu is continually being recharged with methane by the ongoing tectonic activity.

WEATHER AND CLIMATE

Due to its location, just two degrees from the equator, Rwanda receives direct sunshine all year-round. The average daily temperature is 75°F (24°C), and temperatures vary little during the year. High- and low-temperature extremes are unknown in the inhabited portions of the country. Day to day and season to season, conditions remain basically the same: monotonous. The country does, however, experience some seasonal differences in its weather. It has two wet seasons and two dry seasons. October to November is the short wet season, but the main rainy season lasts from March until the end of May. The dry seasons last from December to the end of February and from June to the end of August. Located on the central plateau, Rwanda's capital, Kigali, averages about 40 inches (100 centimeters) of rainfall annually and experiences a mean annual temperature of 66°F (19°C). Conditions in the uplands are so pleasant that many people refer to them as resembling an eternal spring.

Kigali, the capital and largest urban center of Rwanda, is home to about 600,000 residents. Unemployment is high and social services are lacking, including water supply, power provision, and sewerage services.

POPULATION GROWTH AND ENVIRONMENTAL DEGRADATON

Rwanda's physical geography and demography (the statistical study of the human population) have created major environmental challenges. Population growth has outpaced food production, mostly due to lack of available land to put into cultivation. Consequently, intensive crop cultivation is practiced on unsuitable land for farming, or land that should remain fallow for long periods of time. Almost every slope in Rwanda is intensively cultivated, including very steep slopes. As a result, rainfall often washes away both crops and the soil itself. In the northwestern territory, where the potential for agricultural productivity is high, the expansion of agriculture onto marginal lands has produced serious slope failures.

While intensive cultivation is the norm throughout Rwanda, it is particularly extreme in areas with extensive fragmentation. (Many farms have been subdivided numerous times as they pass from one generation to another.) In a number of areas, the inherited farm lots average less than three acres (1.2 hectares) and are much too small to support a family. Farmers try to grow more than one crop on the same land in very short cycles. The results are poor yields, soil exhaustion, malnutrition, hunger, and extreme frustration.

In the eastern part of the country where swamps and wetlands predominate, agriculture destroyed the wetlands and produced flooding and loss of wildlife habitats. Population pressures have taken a sharp toll on Rwanda's forested land area. In 2000, about 30 percent of the country was covered by dense forest; today the figure is about seven percent of the total land area. Throughout the country, high fuel-wood consumption is producing rapid deforestation of the remaining natural forests. Woodland is cleared for farming, and lumber is used widely in construction. Additionally, wood remains the primary fuel used in many, if not most, homes for cooking and heating.

The degradation of Rwanda's resource base is closely tied to pressure exerted on limited farmland by a large and rapidly growing population. Fully 90 percent of all Rwandans depend upon agriculture for their survival. Until the genocide, Rwanda's population was growing at a rate of 3.7 percent per year, resulting in relentless pressure on lands for farming, raising livestock, and other agricultural production. Converting pastureland into cropland decreased the production of manure, and thus, decreased soil fertility. Virtually all available land in Rwanda is already being used, with the exception of two subregions, the Nyabarngo Valley and Akagera Park. Thus, rapid population growth usually coincided with shorter fallow periods and increased number of crops, both of which further sapped the soil of its nutrients.

Rwanda's remaining natural forests have a high degree of biodiversity and are home to a number of rare animal species. Increasingly, however, both are threatened by the encroachment of refugees fleeing the numerous conflicts in the region. The Nyungwe National Forest Reserve is haven to at least 190 species of trees, 275 species of birds, and 12 species of primates. Yet it has felt the effects of population pressure and civil war. Desperate people have cut down large expanses of forest for firewood, and animals have been poached for food. Systematic game hunting has wiped out all the buffalo and most of the duikers, a forest antelope. After two decades of slaughter, there are fewer than ten (most current estimates place the number at six) elephants left in the Nyungwe Forest.

NATIONAL PARKS AND TOURISM

Rwanda is the bridge between the forest ecosystems of the Congo Basin and the Great Rift Valley to the east. It shares in the biological riches of both worlds, offering a concentration of biodiversity found nowhere else in Africa. These have provided beautiful national parks and forest reserves. Perhaps the best known is the Virunga National Park, home to the mountain gorillas, to which Dian Fossey dedicated her life. Mountain gorillas form the primary attraction of Rwanda's emerging tourism industry. Nyungwe Forest, one of the largest mountain forests in Central Africa, is renowned for its large troops of colobus monkeys and rich variety of orchids. Akagera National Park is a savanna park with elephants, hippos, and crocodiles. There is also a large variety of birds.

GORILLA-NAMING CEREMONY

Before leaving the physical geography of Rwanda, the author has a special treat. We are going to a naming ceremony— a gorilla-naming ceremony! This is very special because mountain gorillas, the major draw in Rwandan tourism, are an endangered species. Thus, each new birth of a mountain gorilla is a major cause for excitement and celebration. Conservation workers and researchers name the gorillas after identifying each one, based on his or her unique characteristics. The public is even invited to propose names for the gorillas. Recently, a special event was held. Rwanda's president, Paul Kagame, and his wife named a set of twin gorilla babies that were born in May 2004. The birth of the twins, only the third in recorded history, was a great delight to conservationists and locals. At the peak of the ceremony, while wildlife officials showed photos of the twin baby gorillas, President Kagame stepped forward and announced their names to a wild applause. Their names are *Byishimo*, meaning "happiness," and *Impano*, or "gift." Other names assigned today include *Kunga*, or "peacemaker," *Isoni*, or "shy," and *Kubana*, or "living together." Massive feasting rounds off the ceremony.

The ceremony you will attend includes traditional dances by warriors armed with sticks resembling spears and poems praising development projects financed by revenue from mountain gorilla tracking. Children from villages around the park have proposed several names for the mountain gorilla infants. For Rwanda, conservation of mountain gorillas is more than simply preserving the last of the world's largest primates. Mountain gorillas are the main tourist attraction and provide some measure of healing from the genocide. Gorillas also raise the profile of the country in the eyes of the rest of the world. Officially, tourism is the third leading source of foreign exchange.

3

Rwandan People

Population is one of the most important geographic elements. In studying regions, after all, ultimately all other geographical conditions gain importance mainly in relation to their importance to people. In this chapter, you will learn about Rwanda's population geography and its significance.

DEMOGRAPHIC CHARACTERISTICS

Demography is the statistical study of the human population. Population geography is the area of overlap or interface between geography and demography. Some people actually refer to the study as *geodemography*. In regard to its population, Rwanda is a very tightly packed country. In fact, many social scientists point to the small country's area and huge number of people as being one of its chief problems.

Young people, from birth to age 14, represent 42 percent of the population; adults between the ages of 15 and 64 make up 56 percent of the population, whereas only 2.5 percent of all people are 65 or older. In the United States, by contrast, only 20 percent of the population is 0–14 years, adults 15–64 make up 67 percent of the population, and those aged 65 and older constitute a whopping 12.6 percent. Compared to the United States, Rwanda has a very young population. The median age of Rwandans is 18.6 years, but for the United States it is double that at 36.6 years.

Not only is the Rwandan population younger, but Rwandans do not live as long as Americans. Life expectancy at birth measures the average lifespan of a newborn. It is a good indicator of the overall health of a country. In 2007, Rwanda's life expectancy was 49 years compared to 78 years in the United States. In addition, the infant mortality rate, the number of infants out of every 1,000 born who die before their first birthday, is much higher in Rwanda. Compared to the United States, where only seven out of every 1,000 infants die before they reach one year of age, 85 die in Rwanda.

Nevertheless, Rwanda's population is growing very rapidly, at a rate of about 2.8 percent each year. This is more than double the world's 1.2 percent rate of annual growth, a comparison that clearly points to one of the country's chief problems. Rwanda's very high rate of natural increase (RNI) is due primarily to the large average number of children born to each family. Total fertility rate (TFR) measures the average number of children born to each woman during her childbearing years. In Rwanda, it is 5.4, or more than twice the 2.1 figure for the United States.

Rwanda's population characteristics are typical of developing countries that depend upon subsistence agriculture. To rural families, children are valuable economic assets, because they can perform a variety of chores that help provide for their family's material well-being. Because these families need laborers for farming and other tasks in order to survive, fertility rates tend to be high. Also, since the infant mortality rate tends to be high, many families try to have many children to assure that at least some will survive. Finally, due to widespread poverty, children are the only form of social security for the aged. Thus, most young families try to have as many children as possible in the hope that some of them may survive and succeed in life. They will then take care of their parents in their old age. All

Age/Sex Breakdown of Rwanda's Population (in millions)

AGE	2005			2025		
	TOTAL	MALE	FEMALE	TOTAL	MALE	FEMALE
TOTAL	9,378	4,662	4,716	15,700	7,827	7,873
0–4	1,563	787	776	2,210	1,114	1,096
5–9	1,294	649	645	2,047	1,028	1,019
10–14	1,087	544	544	1,903	954	949
15–19	1,113	557	556	1,697	850	847
20–24	992	495	497	1,448	722	725
25–29	824	412	412	1,235	615	620
30–34	575	293	283	1,022	508	514
35–39	453	237	217	1,006	502	504
40–44	378	195	183	862	431	431
45–49	325	154	171	688	345	343
50–54	251	120	131	465	235	230
55–59	167	75	91	353	179	174
60–64	115	47	68	279	137	142
65–69	96	39	57	219	97	122
70–74	71	29	42	144	63	81
75–79	43	17	26	74	30	44
80–84	21	8	12	33	12	21
85–89	7	3	4	13	4	9
90–94	1	1	1	3	1	2
95–99	0	0	0	0	0	0
100+	0	0	0	0	0	0

Source: U.S. Census Bureau, International Data Base, August 2006 version.

In July 2004, crowds lined the streets as the motorcade of U.S. First Lady Laura Bush and her daughter Jenna traveled through Kigali. They visited Rwanda, South Africa, and Tanzania, including an evangelical church in Kigali that shelters children orphaned by the 1994 genocide and those afflicted with AIDS.

these factors are at work in Rwanda and probably explain the high population growth rate. Moreover, the Roman Catholic Church has strongly opposed population control efforts in Rwanda.

In Rwanda, most of the leading causes of death are avoidable. They include such communicable diseases as malaria, HIV/AIDS, diarrhea, hepatitis A, and typhoid fever. In the United States, on the other hand, leading causes of death are degenerative diseases such as heart disease, stroke, and cancer. Besides HIV/AIDS, which is being controlled quite well for those with access to antiretrovirals, communicable diseases are not a major source of concern in the United States. Three percent of Rwanda's adult population is living with HIV/AIDS, compared to about one percent of the U.S. population that suffers from the disease.

POPULATION DENSITIES

Rwanda's population density is the highest in Africa and one of the highest in the world. In fact, population pressure on land may have been one of the underlying factors of the ethnic conflict. Let us look at this possible link more closely. In considering population density, geographers seek to understand how much land and how many resources are available to support a given population. Too many people in a small area—particularly if they inhabit a less-developed country (LDC)—may lead to crowdedness and insufficient resources such as food and other necessities.

Geographers define population density using two measures related to land area. *Arithmetic density* measures the total number of people per square mile of land. Countries with large total populations, but small land areas, have high arithmetic densities. For example, Japan, with a total land area of 145,900 square miles (377,879 square kilometers) and a 2006 population of 127.9 million people, is very densely populated. In fact, the country's arithmetic density of 877 people per square mile (339 per square kilometer or psk) of land is one of the highest in the world. In contrast, Canada is one of the most sparsely populated countries. With 3.8 million square miles (9,842,000 square kilometers) of land and a total 2006 population of only 32.6 million, the arithmetic density is only 8.4 people per square mile (3.25 psk). The United States has an arithmetic density of 80 per square mile (31 psk), whereas Rwanda's is a staggering 960 people per square mile (370 psk). That is 12 times the population density of the United States and 11 times the density of Sub-Saharan Africa as a whole!

The problem with arithmetic density is that it emphasizes the total amount of land, rather than the amount of land that is suitable for agricultural production. For example, a huge total land area has little use for agriculture if it is mostly arid, rocky, and rugged terrain, as is the case in Rwanda. To capture more precisely the population pressure on agriculturally productive land, geographers define *physiologic density*. This approach to population density is based upon the number of people per unit of land that is suitable for agriculture—land that is good for either growing crops or grazing livestock. The physiologic density of Japan is 8,104 per square mile (3,129 psk) compared to 169 per square mile (65 psk) for Canada, and 448 (173 psk) for the United States. Rwanda has a physiologic density of 2,419 per square mile (934 psk), while the figure for Sub-Saharan Africa is 1,274 (492 psk).

Such shortage of agricultural land can be a source of conflict, particularly when other natural resources are limited or have been overexploited. *Overpopulation* is a value judgment. The concept suggests that the amount of land is inadequate to support the existing population. Many people consider Rwanda overpopulated. *Underpopulation*, on the other hand, is a condition in which, given the available land resources, there are too few people to permit effective exploitation to improve livelihood. In such a situation, population increase is considered desirable. Most experts consider Canada to be underpopulated. However, population density is not directly tied to overpopulation. A country may have a small population density and be overpopulated, or may have a high population density and still be underpopulated. Rwanda, by nearly any measure, is grossly overpopulated.

Carrying capacity measures the number of people an area can support on a sustained basis given the existing capital resources and technology available. For example, a developing country using slash-and-burn agriculture may be unable to support a large population adequately. On the other hand, a country that uses intensive agriculture, including fertilizers and irrigation schemes, may be able to provide adequately for many people. Carrying capacity is usually related to the level of economic development. With a per capita income of $34,510 each year (2006), Japan has a high population density that is matched by a very high level of economic development. In contrast, with only $1,290 per person per year, Rwanda has a high population density and very low level of economic development.

SETTLEMENT PATTERNS IN RWANDA

Rwanda's upland areas are the country's most productive land for farming and herding. As a result, the north-south aligned central plateau is the most densely populated part of the country. Most Rwandans prefer to live in the highlands, where it is cooler and much more pleasant. The volcanic soils of the region tend to be richer. And of great importance, the tsetse fly that causes sleeping sickness, the dreaded disease that kills cattle and can sicken people, is absent. Population densities are low in the western slopes approaching Lake Kivu, but lowest in the eastern lowlands where malaria and other tropical diseases are widespread.

Rwanda has a low rate of urbanization. In fact, more than 80 percent of the population lives in rural areas. Kigali, the capital and largest city, is home to only about 300,000 people. Prior to the war in 1994, only 6 percent of the population lived in urban areas. Since the war, however, urbanization has been very rapid, with many returning refugees choosing to live in Kigali instead of their rural homes, many of which were destroyed.

POPULATION PRESSURE AND
LAND FRAGMENTATION

Due to Rwanda's high population density and excessive dependence on agriculture, its rapidly growing rural population

The primary exports of Rwanda are coffee and tea. They are well-suited to the small farms, steep slopes, and cool climates of Rwanda. Tea and coffee production ensures access to foreign exchange, but decreasing farm size continues to be a concern. Here, a worker sprays vermin poison at a tea plantation near Volcanoes National Park (French: Parc National des Volcans).

is farming progressively smaller parcels of land. This process is called land fragmentation. It makes agriculture inefficient, increases rural poverty, and encourages rural-urban migration.

In Gikongoro, formerly a province in southern Rwanda, Yohanna Nkuliye is planting potatoes on a tiny plot of land. Hundreds of tiny plots of land like his stretch along the valley. Yohanna's father farmed this same land. When he died, it was divided between Yohanna and his four brothers. Yohanna himself has six sons who have a claim on his farm. When he dies, they will have to share this plot between them, and each will have an even tinier plot to farm.

"There are more people now and the soil is old. That's why we die of hunger. The land is not enough for my family," he says.

Thomas Malthus, an economist and demographer, proposed a theory in 1798 that essentially states that unchecked population increases in a geometric progression (2, 4, 8, 16 . . .) while food resources increase only at an arithmetic progression (2, 3, 4, 5 . . .). Thus, unless controlled, population growth will exceed the resources needed to support it. When this happens, natural checks such as war, disease, or famine will result. For a long while, many scholars rejected these harsh ideas. New technologies improved agricultural production in revolutionary ways, and food production kept pace with a growing population. Subsequent developments, particularly those happening in many of the world's poorer countries, have caused people to rethink Malthus's ideas. The new theory, called neo-Malthusianism, states that food production may not be a problem. But rapid population growth, they suggest, diverts scarce resources from capital investment into unending social welfare programs such as day care centers and schools, and thus reduces economic growth. To improve living standards, they believe, population growth must be controlled through reduced birthrates. In Rwanda, however, while population control is very much needed, it is unlikely to happen without substantial changes in the economy and technology. Most Rwandans are farmers and need large families to provide farm labor.

Does the Malthusian theory apply to Rwanda? This is a poor country with very rapid population growth. As we have already seen, Rwanda is overpopulated. In fact, according to the United Nations (UN), Rwanda exceeded its carrying capacity in 1985. There were simply too many people to be supported by the country's limited resources. If there were not a shortage of land and other resources in Rwanda, would the ethnic tensions have escalated so easily? That is a good question. But did the shortage of land recruit and arm all those responsible for the genocide? To what extent can we blame the deadly conflict on population pressure? Keep thinking about that. We will answer these questions in Chapter 5 when we discuss Rwanda's history. But first, let us examine the culture, or way of life, of Rwanda's people.

CHAPTER

4

Rwandan Culture

Prior to the genocide, three main groups of people lived in Rwanda. The Hutu, who are mostly farmers, made up 84 percent of the population. The Tutsi, who are mainly cattle herders, accounted for about 15 percent of the people, while the Twa comprised only a handful of the population, about one percent. Although they were three distinct groups and every Rwandan knew which group they belonged to, they all spoke one language, Kinyarwanda. Since the genocide, the Rwandan government has emphasized Rwandan identity. It has implemented measures designed to eliminate ethnic identity, distinctions, and related tensions.

Geographers define a people with a common language, history, ethnic background, and strong sense of group identity as a *nation*. Thus, the Hutu and Tutsi are both nations. A *state*, on the other hand, is a sovereign political entity with a well-defined territory. States with multiple nations are called *multination states.* Those nations that are divided by political boundaries are called *multistate nations.* For example, the Rwandan peoples, Tutsi and Hutu, are multistate nations. Although the bulk of these groups live in Rwanda, large numbers of Hutus and Tutsis live in neighboring Burundi, the Democratic Republic of the Congo, and to a lesser extent, Uganda and Tanzania. A state with only one nation is called a *nation-state.* True nation-states are rare. Japan may be one example.

A common language, religion, and cultural heritage act like a binding force, a glue that unifies people. Geographers call such cultural magnets *centripetal forces.* In contrast, *centrifugal forces* divide people. Multiple languages and religious differences are important centrifugal forces, but can also be centripetal forces. In Canada, for example, French speakers concentrated in Quebec have made several efforts to secede from English-speaking Canada. Language, in this case, is a major cause of dissent unifying those who speak French against those who do not. Similarly, hostilities between Christians and Muslims is a major cause of conflict in many countries. For example, it is an important reason for political instability in Nigeria, where the southern part is predominantly Christian and the northern part is mostly Muslim.

Generally, a common enemy, a national sports team, national anthems and other symbols, and general satisfaction with the government are centripetal forces. Centripetal forces promote nationalism because people take pride in identifying with the state. In contrast, centrifugal forces cause division and may lead to a breakup of the state as people identify more with ethnic or regional groups instead of with the state. Frequently, regional groups demand more autonomy (self-rule) from the central government. Such pressures usually result in devolution—the central government transfers power to such regional groups.

Rwanda is thus an intriguing example of a multination state. The Rwandan people (Hutu and Tutsi) themselves are multistate nations. And, as a result, Rwanda has experienced the negative results of centrifugal forces that culminated in the worst form of genocide. The post-genocide government seeks to promote centripetal forces by encouraging nationalism rather than ethnic identity. The future of Rwanda depends on how effectively these tensions are resolved.

RELIGION IN RWANDA

An overwhelming majority of Rwandans, about 93 percent of them, are Christians. The Roman Catholic Church has the largest following and accounts for about 57 percent of the population. Protestants comprise another 26 percent, Seventh-day Adventists 11 percent, and Muslims make up less than 5 percent. Although Christianity is the dominant religion, most Rwandans practice some form of ancestral worship. Rwandans believe in life after death and see their families as including not only the living, but also the dead and those who are yet to be born. Showing respect to dead family members is considered extremely important. Failing to appease or honor the spirits of dead ancestors through appropriate rituals and offerings will cause the ancestors to inflict curses on the living. Such curses, it is believed, may result in economic hardship, sickness, or even death.

Traditional Rwandan religion has a strong emphasis on fate as opposed to free will. *Imana,* the source of all life and goodness, is the sovereign controller of all events, good and bad. This Supreme Being can only be reached through intermediaries such as the spirits of deceased family members, known as *abazima,* or other illustrious ancestors. In this regard, Ryangombe and Nyabingi are two venerated ancestral deities that can intercede on behalf of the living. Ryangombe is venerated mostly in southern and western Rwanda, and Nyabingi is venerated mostly in northern Rwanda.

Most physical objects are believed to have spirits that serve as intermediaries between the living and the dead. Dead ancestors (abazima) are venerated and revered because they can protect and benefit living family members if they are honored and remembered through sacrifices. Honoring abazima is essential to avoid unpleasant sanctions. Particularly among the Hutu, ancestral spirits often visit with evil intent. Diviners, or fortune-tellers, are believed to have a special connection with the spirit world and act as intermediaries. Hutus frequently use diviners to interpret the wishes of abazima and to recommend ways to appease the malevolent spirits of the dead.

The Rwandan genocide had a profound effect on religious affiliation. The religious landscape, particularly the mix of churches, has changed dramatically. Dozens of new charismatic churches have emerged. Christian denominations such as Seventh-day Adventists and Baptists are growing rapidly. In Kigali, within one year, a church started by Pastor Paul Gitwaza has drawn about 7,000 enthusiastic worshippers during its Sunday service, which lasts about four hours. In Kigali's business district, a daily lunch-hour prayer service is packed to capacity.

Rwanda is a spiritually hungry nation, and its people are seeking help and healing mostly in the new churches. In makeshift church halls and prayer gatherings people are finding strength to cope with their losses. Smaller fellowships and support groups may be more healing for grieving survivors. This is one reason why many people have left the larger, more traditional Catholic Church.

As Pastor Paul explains, "Rwandans are hungry for God. Rwanda is an ambulance carrying sick people. People are looking desperately for a place where they can get a message that can heal their deep wounds, not a repetitive or a traditional belief, which does not touch their hearts. More importantly,

Before the 1994 genocide, an estimated 93 percent of the population was Christian, out of which 57 percent was Catholic. The Roman Catholic Church has experienced a backlash due to the collaboration of some of the clergy in the massacre. There has been an increase in conversions to Islam, which is seen as a less violent religion.

new churches are bringing together Hutus and Tutsis, worshipping side by side, helping heal the nation."

FOOD AND SOCIAL CUSTOMS

The staples of the Rwandan diet include beans, bananas, sweet potatoes, and sorghum. Dairy products, particularly a traditional drink of curdled milk, are also widely consumed. Affluent households consume meat, primarily beef, goat, and chicken. Sorghum and banana beers are common as well.

Serving people food and drink when they visit a home is customary in Rwanda. To show that they are safe for consumption, the host typically sips from the drink and tastes the food first before passing them to the guests. Declining the offered food or drink is considered a grave insult. Visitors are often presented with food as gifts to take with them at the conclusion of their visits.

Rwandans enjoy food and alcohol, including the local sorghum or banana beer, at all important ceremonies such as weddings and funerals. However, full meals are rarely served on such occasions. Each person is served a piece of meat and a roasted potato. A pot of sorghum beer is placed in the center of the room with numerous reed straws, and guests drink from these reeds. Calabashes (large, hard-shelled gourds) of banana beer may also be served.

Being told that one is fat is a compliment, rather than an insult, in Rwanda. The phrase "Tu as grossi!" means "You've put on weight," or the more hard-hitting Rwandan translation "You've gotten FAT!" It essentially means "you look good," or "you look healthy." It points out an essential difference between Rwandan culture and American culture. *Fat* in Rwanda means "beautiful, rich, and healthy"; *thin* means "sick or poor."

The local community traditionally played the primary role in maintaining social order in Rwanda. When crimes were committed or disputes arose, a council of elders would convene to reach a fair settlement in a process known as *agacaca*. This is the process that has been activated as one means of post-genocide reconciliation.

SIGNIFICANCE OF SEVEN AND EIGHT

In Rwanda, the number seven signifies excellence or perfection and has great cultural significance. The seventh child not only receives a special name, *Nyandwi*, but a special ritual as well. A woman who has a seventh child while the previous six are still alive is celebrated as a national hero. She is honored at a special ceremony known as *kwasa indwi*, and may now speak the names of her in-laws without penalty. A warrior who kills seven enemies in the same battle is awarded a special medal called *Umudende* and becomes a national hero.

Due to the value attached to the number seven, the number eight is even more significant. It translates into something, literally, being more than perfect. A newborn baby is named on the eighth day. The eighth baby is also extra-special and given a name that reflects his status. Traditionally, the dowry consists of eight cows. When male children get married and start their own families, they are given *Umunani* ("eight") meaning "inheritance," probably because it was the custom to give eight cows.

COWS IN RWANDAN CULTURE

The cow is central to Rwandan culture. It is a symbol of wealth, and the best gift a person can give. When you want to recognize and acknowledge an extraordinary favor done for you, you might say: "What you did for me, you gave me a cow." In appreciation of what they have done, you may want to give them a cow. If someone saves your life, for example, from drowning, you express your appreciation by giving him or her the most precious gift, a cow.

The cow is thus treasured. It is a sign of great respect, honor, and appreciation. The cow denotes wealth and social status. The more cows a man has, the higher his status in society. During marriage, dowry is paid in cows. Eight cows is the typical dowry paid by the rich. It demonstrates that the groom is wealthy enough to be able to provide generously for the bride.

Cows are kept for their offspring and milk. Even when it dies accidentally, its meat is not eaten. When the bride's family receives eight cows as dowry they guard them closely, counting the offspring, which are considered a special blessing.

To show how important cows are, they are considered like military companies. Wherever there is a military parade there is also a corresponding cow parade. The military company has its

The Rwandan government and Send a Cow, a Christian charity, have developed a program aimed at eradicating poverty within individual households by giving productive livestock to at least 600,000 poor families by 2017. This program—One Family-One Cow—trains families in animal management, sustainable farming, and group work. Families also receive ongoing support.

name and so does the cow company. Whenever an important dignitary comes to visit, there is a military parade and a cow parade. Cow parades remain an important part of Rwandan weddings.

Rwandans almost never kill their cows for meat. Only an occasional young bull or sterile cow may be slaughtered. Can you imagine how this cultural value can impact the landscape?

Overgrazing easily becomes an ever-increasing and difficult-to-solve problem. While the number of cattle continues to increase, no additional new lands become available for grazing. Can you imagine the trauma and shock Rwandans experienced during the colonial era when Belgians seized their cows and butchered them for food?

MARRIAGE AND FAMILY IN RWANDA

Marriage is the most basic social institution in Rwanda, and the pressure to marry and have children can be very strong. Most couples select their own mates with parental approval. In northeastern Rwanda, particularly Umutara province, marriage by abduction is common. Local authorities and nongovernmental organizations (NGOs), of course, strongly denounce the practice. Marriage across ethnic lines between Hutu and Tutsi is common, but extremely rare between Twa and other groups. The Twa are generally despised by Hutu and Tutsi alike, who regard them as dirty and dishonest. Polygamy, once extensively practiced, is uncommon except in rural areas of the northwest. Levels of divorce and remarriage are high.

In urban areas, a customary marriage with dowry payment is required before a civil marriage. The dowry is a gift of money or valuables (usually cows) given to the family of the bride by the groom's family; it is a token of appreciation. A man who cannot afford the dowry is not fit to marry. This is required even for Christian marriages. In traditional Rwanda, girls wore crests and shaved their heads when they got married.

CHILDREN IN RWANDAN MARRIAGE

Rwandans consider children a sign of wealth and social standing. They are also viewed as social security for the parents. As one proverb suggests: "The greatest sorrow is to have no children to mourn for you." Consequently, as you learned in Chapter 3, Rwanda has extremely high birth rates, and Rwandan families are quite large.

Within a year of marriage, the newlyweds are expected to have children. In the past, infertility was considered sufficient grounds for divorce. Interestingly, the woman is the one blamed for infertility, never the man. During the marriage ceremony, the bride's family will say: "We're going and will return as soon as you have the baby." The family of the bride takes pride in the birth of children and proudly declares: "We gave you a fertile bride." In contrast, the family of an infertile bride faces stigma and shame. In fact, the bride's family pressures her to have more children, as children are a source of pride. Like cows, children are seen as a blessing—the more the better!

Traditionally, male Tutsi children receive extensive training in public speaking, storytelling, traditional dances, and military skills. Among the agricultural Hutus, children are introduced to farm work quite early. In fact, both boys and girls have assigned chores by the age of five. All Rwandan children are rigidly trained in proper social behavior and in communal and family values. Very important among these values is treating elders with supreme respect and responding promptly and willingly to their commands.

Families live in single-family compounds consisting of several buildings surrounded by a hedge or fence. Each wife (if there is more than one) has her own house in the compound, as do elderly parents. The husband's extended family typically lives in close proximity on the same hill or on a nearby hill.

NAMES AND NAMING CEREMONIES

Names are very important and significant in Rwandan society. They usually provide information about the circumstances in which the baby is born. These may include such events as peacetime or wartime, famine or abundance, and the physical and emotional state of the parents at the time of birth. Many names express patriotism and nationalist ideals. They may refer to such traits as loyalty to the king, fitness to defend the country, acknowledgement of God's greatness, or power and generosity. Others are about cows. In choosing a name for the child, the father typically conveys his beliefs and philosophy, or shares his wisdom and advice about life.

Children are named in a public ceremony eight days after birth. Attending guests comprise family, friends, and their children. After a time of feasting, guests present at the ceremony propose a name for the new baby. Finally, the parents announce the name that they have chosen. More feasting follows the naming ceremony.

Names in traditional Rwandan society were given not only to people but also to animals, objects, and significant events. This is why a naming ceremony for mountain gorillas is a big occasion attracting the attendance of Rwandan president Paul Kagame. For example, disasters such as famine and plague are given names. Here are two illustrations: *Miriam* is the name given to a mysterious disease that killed thousands of cows in the early part of this century. Similarly, *Ruzagayura* is the name of a massive famine that happened during the 1940s.

THE STATUS OF WOMEN IN SOCIETY

Patrilineal (father's side of the family) inheritance is the norm in Rwanda. When a man dies, his sons divide up his land and property. The oldest surviving son cares for his mother and any unmarried sisters. In traditional Rwandan society, women are regarded and treated as dependents of their male relatives. Their fathers, husbands, and male children are expected to manage and protect them all their lives. Thus, the life of a Rwandan woman centers on her position as wife and mother. In fact, the strength of a family is measured in the number of its boys.

Rwandan culture has clear, gender-based roles. Men clear the land, but women do the day-to-day farm work, including planting, weeding, and harvesting. Taking care of livestock is a job for men. In addition, men also do heavy jobs around the house, such as construction, while women run the household, raise children, and prepare food. Women dominate the informal economy such as petty trading, while men dominate formal economic activities.

While things have changed considerably, Rwandan society remains a patriarchy. Men dominate both formally and informally, in education, health, politics, and employment. For example, according to Rwandan law, a wife cannot engage in commercial activity or employment without the approval of her husband. Women are often required to obtain their husband's authorization in order to qualify for credit. Moreover, the law forbids employing women in any job that requires them to work at night.

A RIDE THROUGH KIGALI

Walking along Rwandan streets is a time-consuming, but fun exercise—that is if you enjoy meeting and greeting people. You start out briskly, but don't get far. Every few feet, you see someone you know—a neighbor, cousin, second cousin, or former neighbor. Are you a stranger to the city? Never mind, you get to meet and greet the friends, neighbors, and cousins of your accomplice. Get ready for a long day!

Rwandans almost always shake hands when they meet someone. When greeting someone of higher rank, a person extends his or her right hand while placing the left hand on the right arm as a sign of deference. A typical greeting involves both parties wishing each other large herds of cattle. People stand close together in conversation and often continue holding hands for several minutes after shaking.

If you don't want to greet so many people, you will have to take a motorcycle taxi. There are many of them, they are inexpensive, and they will take you wherever you want to go. If you speak nicely to the owner, you may even get to drive. Or you may sit at the back, wave to the whole world, and enjoy Rwanda's beauty. Just be careful, though. Rwanda's motorcycle-taxi drivers love to speed around potholes and pass people on other motorcycles with baskets full of farm produce on their heads, while cars move in every direction. This is a ride of a lifetime. There's still more of Rwanda to see.

5

Rwanda Through Time

D ue to Rwanda's challenging physical conditions, the region was rather late in being settled. Hilly terrain, dense forests, and swamps infested with malaria-causing mosquitoes made early settlement extremely difficult. Only very determined groups such as slave raiders ventured into this difficult environment. However, three indigenous groups—the Twa, the Hutu, and the Tutsi—did settle the land and establish their homes there.

The Twa arrived first and lived as hunters and gatherers. They were followed by the Hutu, a Bantu-farming people who raised cattle, goats, and chickens. They lived in small fenced enclosures in huts that usually doubled as grain stores. The Tutsi were the last to arrive. Originating from the upper Nile Valley, they came in search of pasture for their long-horned cattle. For the Tutsi, cattle were a status symbol and sign of wealth.

These three groups lived in relative harmony, spoke the same language, and intermingled quite freely. Around the fourteenth century, however, the Tutsi began to consolidate power and expand politically. Gradually they emerged as a dominant minority over the majority Hutu peasants in the resulting political system. Nonetheless, the three groups lived in relative harmony until the Europeans arrived.

COLONIAL ADMINISTRATION POLICIES

Administration styles of the various European colonial powers differed significantly. The British and Germans practiced *indirect rule.* They ruled the colonies through the indigenous leadership, such as local chiefs. Instead of collecting taxes directly, they appointed the local chiefs to collect those taxes, as representatives of the Europeans. In return, the colonists provided protection, a high social status, education, and health benefits for these local elite. However, the Europeans remained superior to these African leaders.

The French pursued a policy of *assimilation.* Their goal was to get the indigenous people to adopt French culture. In fact, if they became French enough, through acculturation (the process of cultural assimilation) and education, they could become French citizens and vote in French national elections. Thus, the French tried to raise the natives to the social status of French nationals, and they mixed freely, particularly with the educated natives.

Belgium pursued a policy of exploitation and plunder. They used the indigenous political structure to impose forced labor and ruthless oppression to gain wealth from the colonies. In the Democratic Republic of the Congo (DRC), for example, natives who failed to meet their quota of forced labor (collecting rubber) had their hands chopped off, or their family killed or held hostage. Thus, colonial policy varied with the colonizing country.

COLONIAL ADMINISTRATION IN RWANDA

The first Europeans to visit Rwanda encountered an elaborate, highly centralized feudal system with Tutsi aristocrats and Hutu vassals. The arrangement was based on a hierarchical system of provinces, districts, hills, and neighborhoods. The Tutsi king, or *mwami,* was the omnipotent ruler who delegated power to the chiefs. Provinces were managed by high chiefs who were usually Tutsi. Districts had two chiefs who were usually Tutsi— a land chief who collected agricultural taxes and a cattle chief who collected cattle taxes. Hill chiefs administered the hills and were responsible for landholdings and grazing rights. Hutus, who obeyed orders from the Tutsi monarchy in this strictly controlled hierarchy, generally headed neighborhoods, the lowest level of the hierarchy. The Hutu suffered discrimination and were greatly disadvantaged under this system.

Between 1898 and the World War I (1914–1918), the Germans established a presence in Rwanda, mainly through a network of trading posts. They implemented indirect rule. Thus, the Germans co-opted and ruled through the existing Tutsi-dominated power structure. They supported the Tutsi monarchy and chiefs. Support was based, at least in part, on convincing the leaders that their security and well-being depended on their faithfulness to the Germans. In exchange, the Germans crushed the opponents of these Tutsi leaders.

After World War I, Rwanda came under Belgian rule and experienced plunder and exploitation through the Tutsi leadership. The Belgians considered the Tutsi a superior race that was relatively more civilized, closer to Europeans in physical appearance, and thus more worthy of power and privilege. In contrast, the Hutu were considered primitive, uncivilized, and ignorant, and the Belgians believed they deserved to be treated like slaves. The Tutsi were trained to believe that they were born to dominate and lead others. The Hutu, on the other hand, were repressed, humiliated, and told by everyone that they were inferior. They were exploited by both the whites and the

Tutsi. The Belgians produced identity cards classifying people according to their ethnicity into one of three groups—Tutsi, Hutu, or Twa. Everyone was required to carry an identity card. The Tutsi were given special privileges, including education that was denied to most Hutu. These policies laid the foundation for conflict between the two groups.

Belgian rule was harsh. They used the hill chiefs to demand forced labor from the predominantly Hutu masses for road construction and coffee planting. Routine beatings and other forms of punishment were administered repeatedly to those who failed to comply. The Belgians overlooked the abuses of indigenous Tutsi officials as long as they got the taxes collected, the roads built, and the coffee planted. Colonial Belgian policy thus preserved and strengthened Tutsi superiority. Because Tutsi functionaries ruthlessly enforced the hated colonial policies, Tutsi leaders were associated with the harsh colonial policies and hated by the Hutu.

INDEPENDENCE AND AFTER

When Ghana became independent in 1957, other African countries also began to agitate for freedom from colonial rule. In Rwanda, independence struggles brought turmoil as the Tutsi elite began demanding an end to Belgian colonialism. Infuriated at the Tutsi, the Belgians shifted their allegiance to the Hutu. The Tutsi elite formed a political party, the Union Nationale Rwandaise (UNAR), to press their demand for independence. With Belgian support and encouragement, the Hutu formed another party, the Party of the Hutu Emancipation Movement (PARMEHUTU). Repressed Hutu animosity toward the Tutsi exploded in a Hutu "social revolution" led by the PARMEHUTU in 1959. This revolution became primarily anti-Tutsi, because the tension and violence were directed mostly against the Tutsi population. More than 20,000 Tutsis were killed, and many more fled to neighboring Burundi, Tanzania, and Uganda. After the 1959 revolution, tension and mistrust

This Belgian Congo soldier stands guard over prisoners captured after fierce fighting between Hutu and Tutsi in 1959. The Hutu had long grown resentful of the social and political inequalities of their positions, which had existed since colonial times. Riots erupted, resulting in the overthrow of the monarchy, the slaughter of more than 20,000 Tutsis, and an exodus of some 200,000 Tutsis to neighboring countries.

between Hutu and Tutsi became commonplace. Between 1959 and 1973, an estimated 250,000 to 600,000 people were killed in these conflicts.

In 1961, PARMEHUTU won a majority of the seats in Rwanda's first National Assembly. Immediately, the assembly voted against the return of the Tutsi king and abolished the monarchy, thereby paving the way for independence. On July 1, 1962, Belgium granted Rwanda independence under the leadership of Grégoire Kayibanda, the PARMEHUTU leader. He became Rwanda's first president. PARMEHUTU obtained 78 percent of the votes (35 out of 44 seats), while UNAR (the

Tutsi-dominated party) received 17 percent (7 seats). A simultaneous referendum rejected the monarchy in favor of a republican system of government. The first government comprised members of PARMEHUTU, UNAR, and other parties. But after a brief period of multiparty rule, Rwanda became a one-party state. Thus, Rwanda began as an independent state with firmly entrenched animosities and hatred between the Hutu majority and the minority, but politically dominant, Tutsi.

Grégoire Kayibanda's regime was overthrown in a coup on July 5, 1973, led by another Hutu, Major General Juvenal Habyarimana, the defense minister. He dissolved the National Assembly and the PARMEHUTU Party and abolished all political activity. In 1975, President Habyarimana formed the National Revolutionary Movement for Development (MRND) whose goals were to promote peace, unity, and national development. Under MRND, Rwandans went to the polls in December 1978, overwhelmingly endorsed a new constitution, and confirmed Habyarimana as president. He was reelected again in 1983 and 1988, when he was the sole candidate. Responding to public pressure for political reform, President Habyarimana announced in July 1990 his intention to transform Rwanda's one-party state into a multiparty democracy.

POLITICAL AND ECONOMIC REFUGEES

At the beginning of the 1980s, more than 600,000 Rwandans, mostly Tutsi, were living in the countries surrounding Rwanda. Most were political refugees, but all of them were also economic refugees. In 1982, Uganda expelled thousands of these refugees, but Rwanda sent them back. In 1986, the Rwandan government declared that Rwanda was too overpopulated to permit the return of Rwandan refugees. This infuriated the refugees, who insisted on their right to return home. While the government was negotiating with Uganda about these refugees, Rwandan exiles banded together as the Rwandan Patriotic Front (RPF) and invaded Rwanda from their base in Uganda. They hoped to remove Habyarimana, establish a more democratic government, and assure the return of the refugees. The rebel force was composed primarily of ethnic Tutsis. It blamed the government for failing to democratize and resolve the problems of some 500,000 Tutsi refugees living in exile.

With the help of French and Belgian troops, the Rwandan army repelled the RPF attack. The government accused Tutsis and moderate Hutus of being accomplices of the RPF and arrested or killed several hundred of them. Special security measures were imposed to prevent further attacks. The steps included requiring citizens to participate in patrols at night and to man barriers to monitor traffic on roads and paths. These measures convinced people that there was a real danger of enemy infiltrators. This common enemy became a centripetal force that united Rwandans, particularly the Tutsis and Hutus who were against the RPF. Rwandan military authorities circulated a memorandum that defined the enemy as the Tutsis inside or outside the country and anyone who supported the enemy.

Rwandans—Tutsi as well as Hutu—were frightened by the RPF attack. Tutsis recalled the reprisal killings following invasions by refugee groups in the 1960s and feared they would be targeted again. Hutus remembered the slaughter of tens of thousands of Hutus by Tutsis in neighboring Burundi in 1972, 1988, and 1991 and dreaded the prospect of killings on a similar scale by the RPF. In the 1972 event, an estimated 150,000 Hutus were slaughtered by the Tutsi-led government of Burundi after a failed Hutu insurrection.

Pressured by donor nations to initiate political reform to end the war, Habyarimana lifted the ban on political parties in 1991. Fifteen parties emerged almost immediately. They included the Democratic Republican Movement (Mouvement Démocratique Républicain, MDR), which became the chief threat to the MRND. A group of Hutus established a new party, the Coalition for the Defense of the Republic (Coalition pour la Défense de la République, CDR). The CDR was anti-Tutsi. All the parties organized youth wings, which increasingly engaged in violence against rivals. The MDR youth wing, the *Inkuba,* or "Thunder," harassed MRND supporters. In response, the MRND youth group, the *Interahamwe,* was transformed into an armed militia with training from regular soldiers beginning in 1992.

After further clashes, the RPF and Rwandan government signed a cease-fire at Arusha, Tanzania, in July 1992. The agreement was brokered by the Organization of African Unity (OAU), which agreed to send a small force to monitor the cease-fire. It established a timetable to end the fighting and engage in political talks, and it also arranged for power sharing. The cease-fire took effect on July 31, 1992, and political talks began on August 10, 1992. However, intermittent violence persisted and eventually exploded in the 1994 genocide.

ECONOMIC CONTRIBUTORS TO THE GENOCIDE

The economic system Rwanda inherited at independence was an important factor in the Rwandan crisis. Unlike other countries with multiple sources of foreign exchange, at independence coffee provided 80 percent of Rwanda's foreign exchange earnings. Thus, the slightest change in coffee prices had major implications for Rwanda.

Poverty levels were high. Due to acute demographic pressures (including 3.2 percent yearly population growth at the time), land fragmentation, and soil erosion, the economy was particularly fragile in rural Rwanda. Yet Rwanda was self-sufficient in food production, and until the late 1980s, food imports were minimal.

Rwanda's economy experienced severe difficulties in the 1980s. When world coffee prices plummeted by more than 50 percent, Rwandan farmers were crushed, as was the country's economy. Widespread famines erupted. Desperate, Rwanda appealed to the World Bank and was forced to accept the agency's structural adjustment program.

Between 1989 and 1993, when Rwanda began to implement structural adjustment, life was extremely difficult. Many changes imposed by the World Bank shocked the economy. Trade was liberalized, and many state businesses were privatized. Government subsidies on health and agriculture were removed. Many government employees were laid off. Rwanda's currency was devalued. Immediately, the Rwandan franc lost half of its value, inflation skyrocketed, and public services collapsed. Food shortages emerged, particularly in rural areas, and an outbreak of malaria swept the country. Despite soaring domestic prices, coffee prices remained at the low 1989 price. In desperation, some farmers uprooted coffee trees to make room for food crops. But it was too little, too late.

The farmers were miserable. Coffee income had been almost erased, yet there was no viable economic alternative. Due to the removal of government subsidies, the prices of farm inputs such as fertilizer were extremely high. At the same time, trade liberalization meant that relatively cheap food imports and food aid were flooding the Rwandan market. This made it even more difficult for Rwandan farmers to compete. Famine became widespread in the southern provinces.

Government workers had been equally devastated. For those who still had jobs, the devaluation and high inflation meant that their salaries could only buy a fraction of what they had in the past. The massive layoffs meant a huge pool of unemployed young men who were ready to do anything to survive or make a living. Capitalizing on this excess labor, the Rwandan army increased its size from 5,000 to 40,000 in 1990. Perceptions of crime and insecurity became widespread. When the foreign loans started to flow into Rwanda, small weapons were the most popular purchase items. Farmers who had lost their farms, wandering youth, and the urban unemployed joined the ranks of the militias. Thus, the economic crisis and

Rwanda has one of the highest population densities in Africa, and 90 percent of its residents depend on subsistence agriculture. Small plots of land, erratic rainfall, decreasing soil fertility, and the low usage and high cost of agricultural inputs (such as pesticides, mechanized equipment, labor, and fertilizer) result in about 10 to 12 percent of the population suffering from a food shortage every year. Here, women receive food at a distribution center.

the associated desperation provided a perfect setting for the events of 1994.

THE GENOCIDE

On April 6, 1994, the airplane carrying President Habyarimana and the president of Burundi was shot down as it prepared to land at Kigali. Both presidents were killed. As if on cue, military and militia groups began rounding up and killing Tutsis and political moderates. The presidential guard immediately murdered the leaders of the political opposition, and the slaughter of Tutsis and moderate Hutus began. Encouraged by the presidential guard and radio propaganda, the Hutu military and militias, especially the Interahamwe, attacked Tutsis wherever they found them. Soldiers and police officers encouraged or forced Hutu civilians to murder their Tutsi neighbors. Participants were rewarded with money or food, and some were even told they could appropriate the land of the Tutsis they killed. Between April and June 1994, an estimated 800,000 Rwandans were killed within 100 days. Most of the dead were Tutsis and Hutu moderates.

Amazingly, the world (including the United States) stood by watching passively. In fact, the United Nations withdrew its troops after 10 Belgian soldiers were killed. France and Belgium sent troops to evacuate their citizens and other expatriates but left Rwandans to their fate. Rwanda was in flames.

Stories of the atrocities that occurred during this time are sometimes too difficult to comprehend. An example is the following atrocity reported by Human Rights Watch: A Hutu woman married to a Tutsi had taken refuge in a church with their 11 children. The Hutu killers asked her to choose between dying with her husband and living with her children. The children, classified as Tutsi because their father was Tutsi, would not ordinarily have been allowed to live, but the assailants had said that they would be allowed to depart safely if she agreed to go with them. When she stepped out of the door of the

On April 6, 1994, President Juvenal Habyarimana's plane was shot down, killing him (a Hutu), President Ntaryamira of Burundi, and several others. The assassination of the Rwandan president ignited ethnic tensions that led up to the massacre of almost one million Tutsis and moderate Hutus.

church, 8 of the 11 children were struck down before her eyes. The youngest, a child of three, begged for his life after seeing his brothers and sisters slain. "Please don't kill me," he said. "I'll never be Tutsi again." He was killed with his mother.

RWANDA AND THE UNITED NATIONS: WHY WAS THE WORLD SILENT?

The tragedy is remembered as the worst example of genocide in the twentieth century—about one million people butchered during a period of 100 days! Even more difficult to comprehend is the apathy of the rest of the world. Literally, the world watched as Rwandans killed Rwandans, brutally decimating the Tutsi and moderate-Hutu population. The UN and the United States did nothing to avert the genocide, or to stop it once it started. Although appalling atrocities were committed by militia and the armed forces, the world did nothing. Why?

Shortly after the beginning of the genocide, European countries with nationals in Rwanda began immediate repatriation of their citizens. The foreign troop buildup was substantial. It included about 500 Belgian parachute commandos, 450 French and 80 Italian troops from parachute regiments, another 500 Belgian parachute commandos on standby in Kenya, 250 U.S. Rangers on standby in Burundi, and 800 more French troops on standby in the region. They deployed quickly, evacuated foreign nationals, and left immediately after their evacuation mission was completed. No attempt was made to protect Rwandans at risk.

Why did the United States fail to act? The reason for America's inaction can be traced back to events in Somalia a year earlier and American public opinion. In October 1993, 18 American soldiers were killed in Mogadishu, Somalia, during a UN humanitarian-assistance program. Their helicopter was shot down, and wounded American soldiers were captured, dragged in the streets, and killed. Their torture and humiliation was televised live. Infuriated and shocked at these events, American public opinion strongly opposed any further U.S. participation in UN intervention efforts.

In direct response to these events that were captured in the movie *Black Hawk Down*, the U.S. government decided to no longer participate in any UN military missions. Furthermore, the Clinton administration decided that no significant UN missions were to be allowed at all, even if American troops would not be involved. These were the events that preceded the Rwandan genocide and kept the United States from acting.

Consequently, after 100 days of genocide, not a single reinforcement of UN troops or military supplies had reached Rwanda. U.S. president Bill Clinton later apologized for not doing more to stop the genocide. He claimed that his administration had not been aware of the real situation in Rwanda.

Why did the UN fail to act? At the beginning of the genocide, there was a small UN peacekeeping contingent in Rwanda called the United Nations Assistance Mission for Rwanda (UNAMIR) that numbered only 2,500. The UNAMIR was not planned or deployed to handle the huge mess that Rwanda became after the outbreak of violence. Many of the soldiers were poorly trained and lacked equipment and discipline. Even more important, they did not receive adequate support and direction from the UN. Pressured by the United States, many countries were reluctant to contribute troops to the Rwandan mission.

The day after the Rwandan president's plane was shot down, 10 Belgian peacekeepers, part of the UN mission, were captured and killed by Rwandan government troops. In response, Belgium withdrew all its troops from the UN mission. In addition, Belgium vigorously lobbied the UN to disband the Rwanda mission completely. In response, led by the United States and the United Kingdom, the UN Security Council voted to reduce the UNAMIR troop size from 2,500 to 270. Most countries withdrew all their troops. Only two countries, Ghana and Tunisia, allowed their troops to remain throughout the terrible weeks of the genocide. With such a small contingent, all they could do was to protect themselves.

The UN failed Rwanda because it lacks a standing army and depends on member states to contribute troops when needed. Political will to intervene aggressively in Rwanda was lacking because Rwanda was not strategically important to the United States and other key players of the UN.

Looking back, that was a huge mistake. Hundreds of thousands of people died needlessly. During a recent visit

The human skulls and bones of the genocide victims sit in piles at a memorial site in Murambi. Over 48 hours, an estimated 40,000 victims perished in Murambi alone in April 1994. Survivors have preserved some of the bodies in lime as a stark memorial and warning to the world.

to Rwanda, former president Bill Clinton apologized for his administration's failure to intervene during the 1994 genocide. "The United States just blew it in Rwanda," he said flatly. Rwanda's president, Paul Kagame, accepted Clinton's repeated apologies. Clinton's global AIDS work is a form of redemption for what he failed to accomplish for Rwanda as U.S. president. Clinton's administration fought too long to protect the patent rights of pharmaceutical companies against countries trying to make or import cheaper AIDS medicines.

France has been widely blamed for the Rwandan genocide. French officials were senior advisers to the Rwandan government in the years leading to the genocide. France also provided support arms to the Hutu government. After six weeks of genocide, France, which offered no troops to the UN mission, suddenly decided to intervene in Rwanda. Within a week of the decision, France deployed 2,500 men with 100 armored personnel carriers, 10 helicopters, and other weapons. Although the French forces created a safe haven in the southwest of the country, it was too little, too late.

The Roman Catholic Church in Rwanda has also been blamed for the carnage. Not only did it fail to denounce the government's increasing use of violence against the Tutsi or denounce the genocide, it also failed to apologize for the many clergy who aided the killers.

RWANDA AND BURUNDI: FRIENDS OR ENEMIES?

In many ways, Rwanda and Burundi are so similar that they could be one country. They have the same mix of people—Hutu, Tutsi, and Twa. Both countries have suffered from ethnic conflict and genocide, are extremely densely populated, produce the same crops, and share similar bloody histories. One difference is that whereas in Rwanda, the Hutu have been the aggressor and Tutsi the victim, in Burundi, the reverse has been true. There, the Tutsi have been the aggressor and the Hutu the victims of genocide. Events in one country usually trigger events in the other.

Rwanda and Burundi share a common colonial history. In 1885, Germany declared present-day Burundi and Rwanda part of its sphere of influence. The territory was called German East Africa, and it united the two countries under a single government. Belgium eventually took control of the land from the Germans, and the League of Nations declared it a Belgian mandate known as Ruanda-Urundi in 1923. At independence in 1962, Burundi was led by the Tutsi-led Union for National Progress and Unity (UPONA). The first prime minister, Louis Rwagasore, was assassinated a few weeks after the election and was succeeded by his brother-in-law, Andre Muhirwa.

Anti-Tutsi sentiment began to intensify among the Hutu in Burundi. In a 1964 election, a Hutu won the popular vote, but the Tutsi refused to accept a Hutu prime minister. In 1965, a Hutu rebellion was put down violently. A coup in 1966 replaced the monarchy with a military government and resulted in further Hutu deaths. A civil war that began in 1971 caused some Tutsi deaths in addition to the Hutu toll of about 150,000 dead and 100,000 displaced or homeless. Another coup in 1976 left the country with a one-party government and the coup's leader, Jean-Baptiste Bagaza, as president. Bagaza's regime harbored suspicion toward Catholics, who were considered dangerously sympathetic to the Hutu. In 1986, the government seized control of the seminaries, banned Catholic prayer meetings, and arrested and jailed several priests.

Major Pierre Buyoya led another coup in 1987. Twenty thousand Hutus were killed in the ongoing ethnic conflict the following year. As president, Buyoya attempted to make peace between the two groups, including representatives of both parties in the cabinet. In 1992, a new constitution established a multiparty system, and Melchior Ndadaye, the nation's first Hutu ruler, was elected president. Five months after assuming office, Ndadaye and several other Hutu leaders were assassinated in a failed coup attempt. A further outbreak of violence followed, resulting in some 150,000 Hutus and Tutsis being killed during a two-month period. Another estimated 80,000 fled the country.

Burundi's next president, a Hutu, Cyprien Ntaryamira, and Juvenal Habyarimana, the president of Rwanda, died in a plane crash under suspicious circumstances. The next president, Sylvestre Ntibantunganya, held office for two years. He was removed in a 1996 coup by the Tutsi that installed Pierre Buyoya as president again. The rest of the world responded with trade sanctions, but despite crippling the economy, these sanctions had no effect on the bloodshed. In fact, the bloodshed that started in 1993 continued and the peace process was suspended. In 1999, the sanctions were lifted, and South Africa's Nelson Mandela was appointed as moderator of the peace talks.

Despite a similar history, relations between Rwanda and Burundi remain a complex paradox. While they agree on many issues, they both remain internally fractured and complementary in their conflicts and aggression. An outbreak of violence against Hutus in Burundi means a surge in Hutu refugees fleeing to Rwanda. This, in turn, is typically followed by an outbreak of violence against Tutsis in Rwanda, which sends Tutsis fleeing in all directions, but especially to Burundi. Lasting peace is needed between these countries, but even more importantly between these peoples.

Despite this bloody past, Rwandans—regardless of their ethnic ties—have done a fine job coming together, reconciling their differences, and healing. Today they are working hard to rebuild their country. In the next chapter we will explore how the Rwandan government addressed the many challenges that faced the country emerging from genocide. How do you govern a country grieving the loss of thousands of its citizens? Get ready for Rwanda's success story.

6

Rwanda After Genocide

The events of 1994 changed Rwanda forever. About one million people had been killed in 100 days! Violence and anger was still smoldering. Women, and especially children, had been traumatized, and the gender balance had changed drastically. Millions of people had fled the country and were refugees in neighboring lands. Everybody seemed to have forgotten Rwanda as Rwandans went searching for God and tried to heal. The economy was in shambles. How do you govern such a country? Where do you start? Unfortunately, more bloodshed was still ahead.

Many fled to neighboring Uganda or the Democratic Republic of the Congo (DRC), because they feared retribution by the Tutsi-led government. The Interahamwe forced others to leave because they did not want the victorious Tutsis to govern any Hutus. Refugees settled in camps provided by the United Nations High Commission for Refugees or wherever they could find some shelter. Rwandan refugees included the extremist Hutu militia who had perpetrated the genocide, former members of the Rwandan Armed Forces (ex-FAR), and women and children.

RWANDAN REFUGEES IN EASTERN DRC

An estimated 1.1 million refugees settled in eastern DRC, an area occupied by the Banyamulenge. The Banyamulenge are ethnic Congolese Tutsis who are frequently persecuted because the DRC government refuses to recognize them as citizens. There is speculation that they are Rwandan Tutsis who moved to the Congo during the 1959 Hutu revolution.

The arrival of Hutu refugees immediately set off conflict between the Banyamulenge and Interahamwhe. The better-armed Interahamwe took control of most of the refugee camps of eastern DRC. From these camps, they continued to launch attacks against the Rwandan government. The cross-border raids became a serious problem, and the Rwandan government was infuriated that the DRC government did nothing to stop the invasions. In addition, Congolese troops attacked Rwandan refugees to force them back into Rwanda.

Rwanda decided to invade the DRC to remove the government of President Mobutu, crush the Interahamwe and ex-FAR, and end the Hutu menace. Replacing the Mobutu government with a friendly one, they reasoned, would stop the roaming bands of extremist Hutus operating freely from the DRC. The Rwandan Tutsi-led government also wanted to stop the exclusion and persecution of Banyamulenge.

WAR IN THE DRC

Assisted by Uganda, which also had problems with the Congo, Rwanda and Congolese opposition forces led by Laurent Kabila toppled the Mobutu government in 1997. As president, however, Kabila did not disarm and expel the Hutu Interahamwe and other rebel groups operating from the DRC as Rwanda and Uganda wanted. Interahamwe raids into Rwandan territory

After the genocide, Hutu militias continued to launch attacks while hiding in the Congo's jungles and in refugee camps. This led to a civil war between 8 African nations and 25 armed groups. More than 1,000 people died each day as a result of the war, disease, and starvation. These women (above) have set up a makeshift kitchen while waiting for transportation out of war-torn Kisangani, Congo, in July 2000.

continued. Moreover, the Banyamulenge problem remained unresolved. Consequently, in August 1998, Rwanda and Uganda went to war against the DRC, this time to remove Kabila from power. They accused the Kabila government of equipping and supporting Hutu extremists. To defend his country, Laurent Kabila received assistance from Zimbabwe, Namibia, Angola, and Chad. What has been called Africa's World War had just begun.

Burundi also joined the war on behalf of Rwanda and Uganda. Can you guess why? Similar to Rwanda, Burundi has a Tutsi-led army and government, ruling a Hutu majority population. Burundi had suffered repeatedly from extremist Hutu rebel invasions originating from the DRC. Driving the Hutu militias out of the Congo would end their raids. The stage was set for more violence resulting in widespread destruction and loss of human life.

This is an intriguing example of what geographers call *irredentism*. Where nation group boundaries transcend national political boundaries (multistate nations), conflict easily spills over from one country to the next. Ethnic solidarity becomes a powerful source of violence in multiple countries. An action-reaction pattern develops, and victims in one area become aggressors in the other. Tutsis in Rwanda led the fight against the DRC, while Hutus in the DRC fought against Rwanda and Burundi.

Rwanda's two wars with the DRC and other countries left at least 4 million people dead through violence, disease, and starvation. Before it was all over, however, Rwanda and Uganda were fighting each other in eastern DRC. That was a war within a war. Why will two neighboring countries, with similar people, fight each other in another country?

THE RESOURCE CURSE

Have you heard about the resource curse? Generally, natural resources such as oil and diamonds are supposed to make the countries that have them wealthy. By extracting and selling such resources, a country not only provides jobs for its citizens, but it also can afford to buy products and services from other countries. Countries that lack such resources are usually poor. They have to buy from other countries, but have little money to pay for goods.

Amazingly, the story is not that simple. Having an abundance of natural resources does not necessarily make countries rich. In fact, the reverse is often true. Many countries that have abundant natural resources are overwhelmed with poverty, chaos, war, and political instability. Typically, the scramble for the resource usually leads to fighting. Rebel groups seeking to overthrow the government occupy the resource area, exploit it, and use the proceeds to fund their attacks. Instead of a blessing, the resource becomes a curse. This is the story behind diamonds in Sierra Leone that was captured in the movie *Blood Diamonds*. It is also the story of the DRC and the reason behind the Rwanda-Uganda war in that country.

According to the UN Security Council, global demand for coltan, which abounds in massive quantities in the eastern DRC, is one reason for the Rwanda-Uganda war. Unlike Rwanda, which is extremely poor in natural resources, the DRC has abundant natural riches including gold, diamonds, and coltan (an ore used in laptops and cell phones). Unfortunately, the DRC has suffered massively because of outside struggles for these rich resources. Armed forces from Rwanda, Uganda, and Burundi smuggle coltan from the DRC, export it, and use the revenues to support the war. In 1999 and 2000, Uganda and Rwanda fought each other for control of Kisangani, a large city in Congo's rich diamond fields. Hundreds of Congolese were killed in the crossfire.

During the war, Rwanda began to see rapid economic growth while the DRC descended into chaos that killed an estimated 30,000 people each month. According to the UN, the Rwandan army was exporting at least 100 tons of coltan per month with a monthly value of about $20 million. During a period of 18 months, the Rwandan military is estimated to have made about $250 million from the sale of coltan, even though the mineral is not mined in Rwanda! Also, the volume of Rwanda's diamond exports rose from about 166 carats in

1998 to some 30,500 in 2000—a 184-fold increase! But life in Rwanda was still very difficult.

EFFECTS OF THE GENOCIDE

Life among the refugees in the DRC and other places was extremely difficult. Food was scarce and sanitation conditions were terrible. But security and safety were the most important things on the minds of most people. Separated from loved ones, unsure whether they were alive or dead, hungry children kept crying for their mothers. Poor sanitation conditions spread diseases, and widespread rape and other forms of violence were the norm. Let us meet a young former refugee and hear her story.

Refugee Stories

Six-year-old Genevieve Mahuro fled to the DRC accompanied by her mother, three sisters, and two brothers. Her father stayed behind. As soon as they crossed the border, some armed people fired on them and they all scattered, looking for safety. She did not see her family again. Genevieve thought they had all been killed. She followed other people through the forest, hiding from killers, eating very little, and sleeping under trees or any other available shelter. After wandering in the forest for weeks, Genevieve was found by members of a religious organization, World Vision, and taken to a foster family in a nearby village. The older people were taken to a refugee camp. When the Red Cross visited her village and heard her story, they began to search for her family. She especially missed her father. Using what information Genevieve could remember about her address, they set off to find her father. After a very long time, they found that her father was alive. Her two older brothers, who had been with her in the DRC before they were separated, had managed to return to Rwanda by themselves. Their reunion was a happy one, tinged with sadness. Their

Over one million children are orphaned as a result of the genocide and disease, and 65,000 are heads of households. Girls, some as young as 12, are typically head of households, and most of them must quit school in order to raise several siblings.

mother and two sisters had been killed. Genevieve does not like to talk about her painful experiences in the camps. They make her cry.

Child Soldiers and Genocide

Child soldiers were used extensively in Rwanda's wars. Some were kidnapped and forced to join the fighting, and others joined because they were promised food, clothes, and money.

All of them were forced to kill. The Rwandan Patriotic Front (RPF) used as many as 5000 *kadogo*, or child soldiers. A 1996 Rwandan government study found that 2,600 of them were less than 15 years of age at the time of their military service. After the war, the Rwandan government established a kadogo school. Some 3,000 children received education, material assistance, and help with finding their families. Some later attended secondary school at government expense.

Let us meet one of these kadogo. Gilbert left primary school in 1993, before he turned 14, to join the RPF. He killed at least three people as a child soldier. When the war ended in 1994, he returned to his home in Gitarama, where he learned that his parents had been killed and their house destroyed. Gilbert said that he deeply regrets having killed people and has suffered from depression. He tried to live with his older sister, who is married and has a family of her own, but things did not work out. So he went to live on the streets. He had no place to live, felt alone, and several times wanted to commit suicide. Today, thanks to a Christian charity group, Gilbert is in college. He wants to be a doctor, to heal people and stop the pain of the Rwandan people. He still has nightmares of the attacks, the violence, and the desperation. But Gilbert wants to make a difference, a very positive difference.

Gender and Genocide

During the Rwandan genocide, rape and other forms of violence were directed primarily against Tutsis. Generally, the men were killed and the women raped as a means of shaming the Tutsi. Many women were killed immediately after being raped. Tutsi women were raped after they had witnessed the torture and killings of their relatives and the destruction and looting of their homes. Some Hutu women were raped because they were married to Tutsi men, protected Tutsis, or were affiliated with the political opposition. Beautiful women and young girls were especially vulnerable. Regardless of ethnicity or political affiliation, such women were targeted by the militia groups and often raped indiscriminately, or kept as sexual slaves.

Victims of sexual abuse during the genocide suffer many health problems, especially HIV/AIDS. Many women, including extremely young girls, became pregnant as a result of rape during the genocide. Such "pregnancies of the war," as they are called, involved major health complications for the mother, particularly among the very young, and resulted in miscarriage. The children born through these pregnancies, known as "children of hate," "unwanted children," or "children of bad memories," number in excess of 5,000. Some women abandoned or killed the children at birth, but others kept them. The decision to keep the child often led to conflict with family and community members who rejected the child.

Marie was captured near Nyarubuye by Hutus who took her as a sex slave and raped her more than 100 times. She contracted HIV/AIDS from her rapists and later discovered that she was pregnant. That baby died of HIV/AIDS, and Marie is now in the final stages of the disease. She says: "I don't know why this happened to me. I was a good person. It wasn't my fault I was born a Tutsi."

Religion and Genocide

Due to the genocide, many Rwandans are turning from the Roman Catholic Church to Islam or Protestant Pentecostal faiths. Before the genocide, an estimated 60 percent of Rwandans were Catholic. When the killings started, thousands of Tutsis fled to churches for sanctuary. But the churches became sites of slaughter. At a Nyarubuye church, the scene of one of the worst cases, more than 7,000 people were slaughtered. While some priests and nuns risked their lives trying to stop the slaughter, others were implicated in the killings. The Catholic Church in Rwanda supported President Juvenal Habyarimana and failed to denounce ethnic hatred during his regime.

As a result, many Catholic survivors are turning to other faiths. An example is 20-year-old Zafran Mukantwari, who was the only person in her family to survive the genocide. Her family was Catholic, and those who killed them were also Catholic. In fact, they worshipped at the same church. When she realized that the people she was praying with killed her parents, she quit and became a Muslim.

Sylvie Isimbi is another example. She was hiding in a Catholic school with her father and other Tutsis during the genocide. When the militias finally broke in, her father was shot and killed. Sylvie watched friends and neighbors from her Catholic church rape and murder. Miraculously, she survived. She now attends one of the new Pentecostal churches.

GOVERNMENT AND POLITICS IN WAR TIMES

After its military victory in July 1994, the RPF organized a transitional coalition government called the Broad Based Government of National Unity. The new government included the existing political parties, but the National Republican Movement for Democracy and Development (MRND) Party was outlawed. The RPF government moved quickly to establish security in the country. It also had to begin the process of national reconciliation, establish courts to try the perpetrators of genocide, and stimulate economic development. The RPF government exercised firm control and repressed political dissent.

The year 2003 was a significant one for democracy in Rwanda. The transitional National Assembly abolished the Democratic Republican Movement (MDR), one of eight political parties participating in the Government of National Unity since 1994. Political figures associated with the MDR, including at least one parliamentarian serving in the National Assembly, disappeared. Rwanda adopted a new constitution that eliminated reference to ethnicity. Presidential and legislative

As a result of overcrowded prisons and slow legal proceedings following the genocide, the Rwandan government launched a new court system called *gacaca*. Based on village tribunals with a mix of conventional Western courts, gacaca courts have jurisdiction over those accused of murder, bodily injury, and property damage. Here, prisoners await the beginning of a gacaca court session related to the 1994 genocide in the town center of Kamonyi.

elections were held, and Paul Kagame claimed a landslide victory in the first presidential elections since the 1994 genocide.

Paul Kagame was born in western Rwanda in 1957, but he grew up in Uganda. His parents fled there to escape Hutu violence during the Hutu revolution when he was only two. He became intelligence chief for Yoweri Museveni, current president of Uganda, who was then fighting to overthrow Uganda's government. As military commander of the RPF, he led the attack that ended the Rwandan genocide. President Kagame claims no ethnic agenda and describes himself as a Rwandan and not a Tutsi. The government tried to emphasize national unity instead of ethnic identity. It removed ethnicity from identification cards.

Rwanda has been relatively stable under Mr. Kagame and the RPF. The government has redrawn Rwanda's political boundaries to eliminate the distinction between ethnic Hutu and Tutsi areas. The new provinces were named after the compass points: North, South, East, and West provinces, and Kigali, the capital. The government seeks to weaken ethnic distinctions by merging the old states into multiethnic areas. Most refugees have come home, and access to education and health services has rapidly increased. In 2006, the government conducted local nonpartisan elections for district mayors and for sector and cell executive committees.

POST-GENOCIDE GENDER RELATIONS

Since the genocide, Rwanda has implemented several initiatives to expand the participation of women in the political system. The new constitution, ratified in May 2003, requires a minimum of 30 percent women in all decision-making posts. It also assigns 30 percent of seats in the Chamber of Deputies for women who are elected to office in an election in which only women can vote. Similar measures assure the election of women at the sector and district levels. In addition, the government created the Ministry for Gender and Women in Development. All these efforts have paid off very well. In March 2004, Rwanda became the country with the highest proportion of female parliamentarians in the world. Women comprised 49 percent of Rwandan parliament, compared to only 16 percent in the United States. Some people attribute this dominance of women in parliament to simple demographics—an estimated 70 percent of Rwandans who survived the genocide were female. In 2007, Rwanda's population was 52 percent female and 48 percent male.

Critics claim that Paul Kagame's government represses free speech and criticism. Prominent critics of the government have been imprisoned or forced into exile. Many Rwandans are afraid to speak out against their government. Although multi-party elections have been held, the ruling RPF is the only major political force. Perceptions remain strong that the government is Tutsi-dominated and Tutsis hold the important posts in the economy. Such political and economic exclusion may increase resentment among Hutus. Rural poverty remains a major problem. How the RPF government responds to demands for greater political freedom and more equity in economic opportunities will determine the future of Rwanda.

7

Living in Rwanda Today

Today life is improving for most Rwandans. Peace has finally come to the long-troubled land. As you learned in the previous chapter, although there remains ample room for improvement, the government is relatively stable. Owing primarily to these two developments, the country's economy is now growing. In Rwanda as elsewhere in the world, economic development provides the foundation upon which so many other quality-of-life elements depend.

A TRADITIONAL ECONOMY

Rwanda's economy depends primarily on small farms and rain-fed agricultural production. It has few natural resources and only a small industrial sector. Ninety percent of the labor force is engaged in agriculture, much of which is at the subsistence level. Only 10 percent of the population is engaged in manufacturing or the economy's service sector, making Rwanda one of the world's most traditional—and impoverished—economies. In this sense, Rwanda provides a classic example of what has been called the *agricultural employment paradox*. Countries with a high proportion of the total labor force engaged in agriculture are more likely to be poor with high rates of malnourishment and starvation. In contrast, countries with few farmers, such as the United States or Canada (both with less than 2 percent of the population engaged in agriculture) are more likely to be rich and well nourished. Such nations depend on mechanized agriculture instead of crude farming tools such as machetes and hoes.

Coffee and tea, Rwanda's main agricultural exports, are suited to the small farms, steep slopes, and cool highland climates. Tourism, based on mountain gorillas, has great potential as a source of revenue. Rwanda is a member of the Common Market for Eastern and Southern Africa (COMESA). Some 34 percent of Rwanda's imports originate in Africa, 90 percent from COMESA countries.

Rwanda's agricultural products roughly follow differences in elevation. The lowest elevation (2,500 to 4,500 feet; 760 to 1,370 meters) is devoted to subsistence crops such as bananas, beans, corn, and plantain. The next level of elevation (between 4,500 and 6,500 feet; 1,370 to 1,980 meters) is the most densely populated and devoted to cash crops such as coffee, tobacco, and potatoes, as well as subsistence crops. The highest elevations (above 6,500 feet, or 1,980 meters) support tea, tobacco, grains such as barley, and flowers.

Rwanda's economy was severely impacted by the war. During the five years of civil war that culminated in the 1994 genocide, the gross domestic product (GDP) declined in three out of five years. GDP is the market value of all goods and services produced in a country in a given period of time, usually one year. In 1994, the GDP declined more than 40 percent, due mainly to lost production. However, in 1995 it grew by 9 percent, primarily as a result of foreign aid Rwanda received. Since 1996, Rwanda has experienced steady economic growth, although it does import more than twice as much as it exports

Rwanda has received outside assistance so that farmers can increase their incomes by diversifying their income sources. The World Bank pledges to train farmers to develop entrepreneurial skills, to manage and share information with others via community Internet centers, and to try innovative farming methods.

each year, resulting in a whopping trade deficit. Despite an open trade policy, a favorable investment climate, cheap and abundant labor, and tax incentives, private foreign investment is low. It appears that foreign investors remain wary of the recent history of war and political instability.

STRUCTURAL ADJUSTMENT IN RWANDA

Rwanda was one of the first African countries to implement a *structural adjustment program* (SAP). When countries are unable to pay their debts and need money, they usually turn to the World Bank and the International Monetary Fund (IMF) for a loan. Before receiving a loan, such countries have to meet

certain requirements. Some of the most common requirements include devaluation of the national currency, removal
of government subsidies, privatization of government enter-
prises, reduction of government employees (through layoffs),
and salary freezes. These measures aim to reduce government
spending. They make exports to foreign countries cheaper (so
they will buy more) and imports more costly. For example, in
1994, in the midst of the genocide, Rwanda implemented a
67 percent devaluation of the national currency. This meant
that overnight, the currency could buy only one-third of what
it used to buy before devaluation. Can you imagine how this
affected Rwandans?

Let us imagine that you have been saving money to buy an
imported bicycle that costs US$150. If the currency were deval-
ued by 50 percent, your bike would now cost US$300. Even if
you do extra chores, it would take you much longer to be able
to buy your bike. This is because a salary freeze means no raises
are allowed. On the other hand, the price of everything—and
particularly imported goods—has increased. Removal of government subsidies means that the cost of such things as health
care, education, and agricultural commodities will increase.
For example, tuition fees may increase. Not only can you not
afford to buy your dream bike, but because your parents are
unable to afford your tuition fees, you may have to drop out of
school. To understand other elements of structural adjustment
and how it impacts people, let us meet the Nsenga Family.

Fifteen-year-old Emmanuel and his sister Rosine live with
their parents, Michael and Yvette Nsenga. Michael is a coffee
farmer, and Yvette is a health worker. Although they are well
off by Rwandan standards, life is not at all easy for the Nsengas.
Michael's coffee farm is less than two acres (0.8 hectare, or ha)
in area. When his father died 20 years ago, his five-acre (2 ha)
plot was divided among his four boys. Michael's older brother,
who had three children of his own, realized after a few years
that he could not support his family on the one acre (0.4 ha)

of hilly terrain he received. So he sold his plot to Michael and moved to Kigali. That is why Michael has two acres. Most people around here have just one.

Every year, Michael dutifully tills his coffee farm. He has planted food crops among the coffee plants, including plantain, cassava, and vegetables, that are mainstays of the family's diet. They also have a few chickens around the farm. When the price of coffee is high, he makes a tidy profit and is able to provide well for his family. In fact, he bought a sewing machine for his wife two years ago. But this year is particularly difficult. Michael compares it to 1993, the year before the genocide. Although he had a good crop, the price of coffee on the world market dropped so low that he could not afford to provide food for his family. That was the year the government increased the prices of everything, including even fertilizer, as part of the structural adjustment program. He could not afford to buy fertilizer for his fields, because it was far too expensive. His wife, Yvette, also lost her job because the government claimed there were too many health workers. That was a very rough year for the Nsenga family.

Michael hopes this year will be different. The price of coffee is low, fertilizer is still expensive, and the rains have been very poor. But he hopes that the new business he has just started, a telecenter where people come to make phone calls and check e-mail messages, will generate enough profit to support them. Very soon, he hopes to be able to leave coffee farming altogether and focus on his new business.

The year 1993 was difficult for Yvette too. Rosine had just been born, and within months of her return from the brief maternity leave, she was sent home with several other health workers because of the structural adjustment policy. She had been saving money to buy a sewing machine. At the time, it sold for the equivalent of US$100. With the devaluation, however, the price changed overnight to about $240. Her hopes dashed, Yvette decided to focus on taking care of Rosine and

Emmanuel. Now with the war behind them and the economy doing so well, she agrees with Michael that they need to move from coffee farming to concentrate on their new business.

As part of structural adjustment, several key firms including Rwandatel, the government-owned, fixed-line provider and the country's second-largest cell phone provider, were sold. Similarly, the government sold off several government-owned tea estates and banks.

RWANDA AS EAST AFRICA'S EMERGING SILICON VALLEY

After the genocide, Rwanda's leaders considered several different strategies to jump-start the economy and accelerate national reconciliation. Rwanda's physical and human geography limited their options. The country is geographically landlocked, resulting in long distances to the closest seaports. Access is made even worse because of the very poor transportation infrastructure in neighboring countries, including the politically unstable DRC and Burundi. Moreover, the cost of air travel is astronomically high—the Nairobi-Kigali route is believed to be one of the most expensive flights per mile in the world. And, of course, the country has very few natural resources, such as petroleum, gold, or diamonds. Terrain is hilly, and in a small country with a large population, there is a shortage of land. After the war, Rwanda seemed to have few options to pursue for economic development. Traditional raw material export trade was not a viable option. The country had little choice but to be different. If you were the president, what would you do?

Rwanda needed to rebuild its infrastructure. But so many people, particularly young males, had been killed in the genocide that the country faced an acute shortage of trained local workers to get the job done. The government made what might seem to many to have been a daring and rather strange (at least for a poorly developed country) choice. It decided to focus on information technology. With foreign assistance, the government also established the Kigali Institute of Science and Technology (KIST) to train technical experts. This institute has graduated thousands of Rwandans now specialized in that field. In fact, the country is now recognized as a leader in the development of biogas technology and renewable energy.

Aiming to become the "Silicon Valley of East Africa," Rwanda invested heavily in information technology. It offered computers and Internet access to young people across the country. Most primary schools now have access to computers, and many secondary schools have wireless Internet access. Moreover, Internet cafes are growing like mushrooms in Kigali and in other major urban centers. Telecenters are bringing rural areas online and promoting e-commerce.

Rwanda's dedication to information technology is unparalleled among developing countries. In January 2007, Rwanda spent 1.6 of its gross domestic product on science and technology. This level of expenditure compares favorably with economically developed countries; most developing nations average less than 0.5 percent. Today thousands of computers are being ordered for schools from Rwanda Computer Network, which has already assembled and sold more than 6,000 "Gorilla 1000" desktop computers to the government and banks. A software firm has translated a free open-source version of Microsoft Office into Kinyarwanda, the main language.

Fortunately, Rwanda has received much help in its high-tech efforts. An excellent example is the assistance contributed by Google. The company has provided free software and engineers to train Rwandans to develop and offer its applications under their own domain names. Google also provides guaranteed service and support to all Rwandan institutions. Besides Google, several other national and supranational organizations are supporting Rwanda's effort. For example, the Rwandan Information Technology Authority (RITA) is wholly sponsored by the Swedish government. The Dutch government paid for

President Paul Kagame believes that Rwanda can become the trade and commercial hub of East and Central Africa. His anti-poverty program includes building a modern transportation network; improving the educational system, especially in science and technology; encouraging private investment; and overseeing all of this with honesty, impartiality, and transparency. His ambitious plans have gained him support from development experts from around the world.

a fiber-optic backbone. Local government portals have been developed, along with a chain of community Internet centers.

As a result of these developments, Internet services are 70 percent cheaper in Rwanda than most other countries. Already Rwanda sells Internet access to Burundi, the DRC and Tanzania for $1,300 per megabit, as opposed to traditional costs of around $4,200. Such developments are a big boost for Rwanda. An indigenous personal computer vendor, Emara, is assembling computers in Rwanda. Using components shipped by a Swedish design firm, Emara hopes to sell these computers in other developing world regions. Consequently, the information technology future of Rwanda is very bright.

The rest of Africa is already taking note. Kigali has also been selected as the headquarters of the 23-country Eastern African Submarine Cable Project, which will greatly increase Internet bandwidth in the region. The telecom mast at the top of the Karisimbi Volcano will serve as a regional air traffic control center.

COFFEE AND RECONCILIATION

The Rwandan government is supporting the establishment of coffee plantations in which Hutus and Tutsis work together. This daily contact will accelerate healing and foster closer relationships in communities. At the same time, it resolves one of the key problems of development in Rwanda—land shortage and fragmentation. It may even resolve the agricultural paradox. By pooling resources, cooperatives are able to invest extra resources and thus have increased production.

Let us go and meet some workers at one of the coffee plantations. Aimee Umuhoza and Beatrice Karigirwa work at a coffee plantation in Kigali, where they pick and clean coffee beans. Aimee, who lost both parents in the genocide, said she needs to work to support her younger brother and sister. While the pay is low, she says the coffee plantation is playing an important role in uniting people. "I have been here for two years, and I can't hate. Even those who killed my parents later died, so why should I create more enmity [bad feelings] by sowing hatred. Here, we are friends because we have the same problems. We understand each other, we don't have any quarrels."

Fellow worker Beatrice Karigirwa's husband and most of her relatives were killed in the genocide. She has one surviving brother who is in the army. She explains that her job gives her hope for a better future and enables her to live peacefully with other women. After the war, she did not want to live with anyone because of what was done to her. But with time, while living with people here, her healing began. She said that hearing the stories of fellow workers, some of whom have no family left, has helped the healing process. Beatrice knows her problems are not the worst. "Coffee," she acknowledges, "has played a big role in the progress of this country. We live in harmony with Rwandans from different areas. If we all stayed at home we would all be thinking in the same way as before, but coming to work in the coffee industry has taught us a lot."

Rwanda has decided to concentrate on specialty coffees, which became popular in the United States and Europe during the 1990s. They are sold through fair-trade deals and bring a premium price on the market, and hence, to growers. Cooperatives are boosting coffee production. Before we leave, let us meet one of the cooperative farmers.

Cooperatives and Coffee Production

Gemima Mukashyaka is a cooperative coffee farmer in Southern Rwanda. After the genocide that killed eight members of her family in 1994, life was very difficult. Everyone was struggling on their own small plots to produce what they could, but it was not easy. To sell to producers, they had to travel long distances. Then a handful of growers formed a team to negotiate with Rwanda's national coffee company. By negotiating as one unit, they got a better price. Many other farmers joined the cooperative, which now has more than 1,500 members and

Rwandan coffee, once considered inferior in the global markets, has now surpassed tea as the country's biggest export, thanks to the Maraba Coffee Cooperative. Through development aid, the cooperative is now self-sufficient and prosperous. Their beans are sold to various roasting companies in the United States and the United Kingdom, including Starbuck's.

supplies coffee to foreign buyers in the United Kingdom. At a time when global coffee prices are in a 30-year slump, such contacts are invaluable.

Participating in the cooperative was a big step for Gemima. She used her profits to hire additional workers and to better provide for her family. She also built a new house and obtained health insurance for her family. The cooperative is helping people to look past the ethnic divisions that split the country. Working with people who suffered as she did from the genocide has brought a strong desire to put the past behind her and to move forward.

HEALTH CARE, HIV/AIDS, AND HEALTH INSURANCE

Only 10 of the world's countries have a more rural population than does Rwanda (80 percent). Yet during the genocide, people felt unsafe in the countryside. As a result, a massive population flow occurred during and after the hostilities of 1994. The result was a considerable increase in Rwanda's urban population. This makes it easier for health-service delivery, compared to the pre-genocide era when most Rwandans lived in small rural settlements. But the health-care system faces a severe shortage of skilled workers. Of Rwandans killed or displaced during the genocide, a disproportionate number were highly skilled and educated members of society, including doctors, nurses, and other health-care workers. As a result, many health centers lack well-trained professionals. In addition, essential physical facilities, equipment, and supplies are scarce. Electricity supply is erratic throughout Rwanda. The unreliable power supply has a very negative impact on hospitals, other health centers, and both research and testing laboratories. Such things as blood safety, data management, and drug storage are all impacted by the erratic electricity supply.

In regard to HIV, Rwanda faces a generalized epidemic. This means HIV is spreading throughout the general population. The dreaded disease is no longer confined to high-risk groups such as sex workers and homosexuals. Its rate of prevalence has remained relatively stable. In fact, since the late twentieth century there has been a slight decline due in part to improved methods of HIV surveillance. Another reason is that many of those who were infected during the genocide have died from the disease. In general, HIV prevalence is higher in urban than in rural areas, and women are at higher risk of HIV infection than are men. Heterosexual sex remains the main means of transmission, and young women ages 15 to 24 are twice as likely to be infected with HIV as young men in the same age group. Populations at higher risk of HIV infection include commercial sex workers and men attending clinics for sexually transmitted infections. While stigma continues to be a problem for people living with HIV/AIDS, effective AIDS education has led to significant improvements.

Before he was diagnosed, Xavier Mdengo's body was racked with endless bouts of malaria, coughing, and lesions that covered his face. He went to the Muhura Health Center in northeastern Rwanda, where he was diagnosed with HIV/AIDS. Fortunately for him, Muhura is one of the few health centers in rural Rwanda that distribute antiretrovirals (medicines). Mdengo, who is 50 and the father of six, began his daily regimen of two pills after taking part in a training course. He said he does not want to think about what his life would have been like without the medicines once the test results established that he was infected with the dreaded disease.

Muhura's distribution of anti-AIDS medicines is part of a government effort to increase the number of Rwandans receiving antiretrovirals. In the past, these medicines were only available in Kigali, and only urban residents and the few rich in rural areas could afford to get them. Despite the government's efforts, the number of rural residents getting the antiretroviral medications remains low. Urban residents continue to have an advantage over the country's rural residents in obtaining life-prolonging medication.

In Muhura, all pregnant women are tested for HIV, and voluntary testing for HIV is very popular for people of all ages and both sexes. If a person tests positive, the patient and an uninfected partner receive training on how to take the medications and prevent further spreading of the disease. They also receive counseling from a social worker. A doctor visits Muhura health center weekly and provides checkups and monthly medication refills. In addition, community health volunteers visit patients each week to make sure they are taking their medications every day. Thanks to the Rwandan government, antiretrovirals are providing hope to HIV patients in rural Rwanda. In addition, the Rwandan government has petitioned the World Trade Organization for permission to import generic HIV/AIDS drugs. Since they are less expensive, success in this effort will bring much needed help to Rwandan HIV/AIDS patients.

One of the most exciting accomplishments of the postgenocide Rwandan government is the establishment of mutual health insurance programs. This has extended health-care coverage to many people who previously lacked access. Participation in the community prepayment health insurance scheme, or *mutuelle,* is available to all Rwandans. All mutuelle members receive services at their designated health center. In the past, widespread poverty kept many Rwandans from seeking health care. Today mutuelle members access family planning and reproductive health services more frequently, as well as preventive care services. Mutuelles are an important tool for unifying the population and providing better quality health care. Supported by Rwanda's Ministry of Health, mutuelles are making a big difference. They have greatly improved the performance of primary health-care providers. Additionally, they are praised for the increased use of health services, particularly much-needed family planning and reproductive health services.

Rwanda still has many huge challenges. Transportation costs remain high and, therefore, pose a burden to the cost of imports and exports. Manufacturing and service industries are desperately needed. Although the tourism industry has potential, support infrastructure–lodging facilities, restaurants, means of transportation, and so forth–is limited. Through the Multilateral Debt Relief Initiative and the Heavily Indebted Poor Country (HIPC) debt initiative, Rwanda has reduced its foreign debt load. Energy needs continue to exert pressure on natural resources, particularly through deforestation. Population growth continues to be a challenge, and diseases such as HIV/AIDS, malaria, and tuberculosis scream for attention.

8

Rwanda Looks Ahead

Although Rwanda has had a difficult and troubled past, the country looks ahead to a hopeful future. Compared with just a few years ago, a drive through Kigali today shows an impressive pace of change. New houses, modern office blocks, and hotels are springing up seemingly everywhere. The Rwandan government appears to be making all the right moves. A new flag and national anthem seek to foster national unity and reconciliation. In addition, to promote goodwill and reconciliation, the government has periodically released prisoners accused of genocide. For example, a total of 60,000 people have been released since 2003, including 8,000 suspects who gained their freedom in 2007. As another gesture of goodwill toward Hutus, Hutu former president Pasteur Bizimungu was released from jail three years into his 15-year sentence through a presidential pardon from President Paul Kagame. Clearly, the future of this beautiful country critically depends upon peace and stability.

RWANDA'S FUTURE AND HIV/AIDS

To address the HIV/AIDS problem, President Kagame invited former U.S. president Bill Clinton and his foundation to assist in developing a comprehensive strategy and action plan in 2002. The resulting plan has made a major impact on the disease. Rwanda has integrated HIV/AIDS care and treatment programs into all levels of central and local government. Antiretroviral therapy has been extended throughout the country. Today it is available to many people who previously could only dream about it.

The Clinton Foundation and other nonprofit organizations such as the Bill Gates Foundation have been good to Rwanda. At Clinton's urging, Dr. Paul Farmer, famous for his work among poor HIV/AIDS patients in rural Haiti, is re-creating his model of AIDS treatment in Rwanda. He has transformed a dilapidated facility that lacked even a doctor into a thriving rural hospital that provides AIDS medicines for more than 1,500 people. Community workers deliver antiretroviral medicines to people with AIDS every day, minimizing reliance on scarce doctors and nurses. With such solid support and the availability of low-cost antiretrovirals, Rwanda is clearly on the path to success in effective control of HIV/AIDS. The strategies developed here may be copied successfully in other African countries.

A TASTE OF RWANDA: STARBUCKS

Thanks to a partnership with the U.S. Agency for International Development (USAID), a taste of Rwanda may only be as far as your local Starbucks outlet. Starbucks markets the brand Rwandan Blue Bourbon. USAID assisted Rwandan farmers in upgrading their coffee-farming and coffee-processing infrastructure. Thanks to this investment, approximately 40,000 Rwandan farmers now have higher incomes and, hopefully, an improved standard of living. These growers aim to produce sustainable quality coffee in sustainable quantities while maintaining standards. They hope to develop a lasting partnership with U.S.-based Starbucks. The government of Rwanda is determined to create a favorable environment for a flourishing relationship and to continue a development strategy that emphasizes public-private sector partnerships.

BIOGAS AND METHANE

Rwanda is pursuing very creative and innovative solutions to a growing energy crisis that has contributed to the problem of widespread deforestation. A major effort is underway to tap the methane (a naturally occurring gas) in Lake Kivu. Another exciting project is the development of biogas. The next time you flush a toilet, consider that you are about to flush away a valuable source of energy. Students like Gilbert Twizere at a secondary school in Rwanda make sure they get a little bit of value for every flush of the school's toilets. With technical guidance from their teachers, they built a biogas chamber that converts their human waste into a much-needed energy supply!

The biogas pit consists of three different chambers. Pipes connect toilets to the main digester, the largest pit. Excess water flows out of the exit chamber, while the compost catches other solid waste. Bacteria break down the waste to produce methane gas that is then piped into the school's kitchen for cooking. It also can run generators to provide electricity.

Twizere and his peers built the chambers using pickaxes, shovels, and wheelbarrows to remove the dirt. The initial cost of 7 million Rwandan francs (US$14,000) for a biogas chamber was eventually earned back through energy savings. Less firewood is used in the kitchens for cooking, and a petrol generator can run entirely on methane gas. The school has established a private company to produce biogas chambers for the market. The company has hired the recent graduates and hopes to build more chambers all over the country. Maybe the next time you flush the toilet in Rwanda, it will not be such a waste. You will actually be providing energy to use in cooking dinner.

Lake Kivu, one of three known exploding lakes, is filled with vast quantities of three dissolved gases—carbon monoxide, hydrogen sulfide, and methane. An explosion could be catastrophic to the 2 million inhabitants that live nearby. Rwanda and the DRC have signed an agreement to extract methane from the lake. They hope not only to produce power for their countries as well as their neighbors, but to also avert a potential natural disaster.

HILLYWOOD, RWANDA'S FILM INDUSTRY

International productions about the Rwandan genocide, such as *Hotel Rwanda*, have led to an exciting new development—a Rwandan film industry. Young Rwandans who worked on these foreign productions are now producing their own films and telling their own stories. And they are succeeding quite well. Kennedy Mazimpaka is an example. He thinks this is timely for Rwanda. "We can't continue to lag behind because we had a genocide. We need to go forward. Right now we need anything that can develop Rwanda. So why not a film industry?"

With these visionaries, Rwandan film is off to a great start and has a big name—"Hillywood." The name, of course, has a familiar ring and also reflects both the beauty of Rwanda and the aspirations of its young filmmakers. Annually, Hillywood holds a film festival on a shoestring budget. Rwandan filmmakers travel throughout Rwanda screening films every evening under the stars. More importantly, these are homemade films. They are made by Rwandan directors and producers and filmed in Rwanda in the local language, Kinyarwanda. One of the most popular films, *Hey, Mr DJ!* is about an arrogant, young DJ who finds out he is HIV positive. The film has charm and a twist of comedy. The crowds love it, but of even greater importance, it provides an excellent opportunity to discuss HIV/AIDS. For many, this was the first time they saw a film in Kinyarwanda. Kids crowded around afterward, eager to find out how they could get into Rwandan film.

Hillywood has been received well outside Rwanda as well. A recent showing at New York Academy of Art hosted dignitaries like former president Bill Clinton and President Paul Kagame. President Kagame welcomed the gathering to a celebration of Rwandan culture, art, and performance. He stated that Rwanda was a country that was healing itself through artistic expression. "The story of the Rwandan film industry is essentially the story of Rwanda itself. It is the story of commitment, resilience and a determination achieving a shared purpose and great progress." In his remarks, Bill Clinton described Rwanda as a miracle. He called attention to the fact that it is one of the most disciplined, well-organized, forward-looking places not just in Africa, but also among all the developing countries of the world. The evening also introduced the works of three extraordinary young filmmakers: Gilbert Ndahayo (*Scars of My Days*), Thierry Dushimirimana (*A Love Letter to My Country*) and Pierre Lalumiere Kayitana (*Behind These Walls*). Next time you feel like a movie, how about trying one of these?

FROM FARMING TO DRESSMAKING

Nyirandeze was widowed during the genocide. The 43-year-old has two living children, 15-year-old Nkurunziza, and 17-year-old

Nyirasafari. Her three other children and husband were killed during the conflict. Nyirandeze grows vegetables on her small plot of land in order to help support her family. Because her farm income is not enough to support them, she also makes beer to sell at the local market every Tuesday and Friday. Without a husband or any other source of support, she could not afford enough food for her family, let alone school uniforms, basic supplies, or textbooks. Although primary education is free, many poor families are unable to buy required uniforms and supplies. Her broken family needed all its members in the daily struggle to survive. Sadly, she had to pull the children out of school. Without an education, the only future she anticipated for them was a bleak one. She feared that they had little to look forward to other than a life full of hard labor on the small plot, or as workers planting, tilling, and harvesting their neighbors' crops. But thanks to one of Rwanda's many nongovernmental organizations (NGOs), the future is quite bright for her children.

Nyirasafari is learning to make clothes in a program run by CARE International. CARE's CHILD project trains community members to teach literacy and vocational skills to older young people who missed out on a formal education. Every morning before class, Nyirasafari rises early enough to fetch water (a one-hour round-trip by foot) and do chores around the house. The classes are held from 8 A.M. until 1 P.M., five days a week. She is learning how to cut material and sew clothing. The classes started with skirts, then dresses, and now students are making shirts. As she proudly models the new blouse she has just completed, she excitedly tells her mom about her future plans. She hopes to get a sewing machine, rent a stall at the market, and make dresses to sell. CARE has worked with district officials to make funds available for "tool kits" for graduates of the vocational program. She hopes to provide food and nice clothes for her family from her job. She expects to save money to buy a plot of land for her mother to grow more crops, like beans,

UNICEF plans to build or repair 1,100 schools and to set up 50 teacher-training centers in Rwanda. Because so many children were unable to attend school for several years, they are now being given a compact version of what they have missed. In addition, Jeanette Kagame, the First Lady of Rwanda, proposed a five-year school campaign focused on retaining girls and getting them from primary into secondary school.

sorghum, and Irish (white) potatoes. Finally, she hopes to teach other children to become tailors.

Nyirandeze beams with satisfaction and pride as she looks at her daughter. "Before, my children could only work as laborers, but from what I see now, the future will be better because they will be self-employed and have permanent jobs instead of working in the fields for the rest of their lives." Like Nyirandeze or Nyirasafari and many other Rwandans, the future is indeed very bright.

A BRIGHT INTERNET FUTURE FOR RWANDA

In terms of information technology, in 2007, parts of Rwanda resembled any advanced, well-developed country. Office workers talk over Skype, the Internet telephone network. With every minister using a laptop computer, cabinet meetings are paperless. This is all part of Vision 2020, the project that seeks to make Rwanda the regional hub of information technology—a kind of "Singapore" of East Africa's Great Lakes. Some donor countries assert that information technology should not be the current main priority of Rwanda. They insist that the government should focus its attention on improving the day-to-day life of the country's rural poor. Government officials, however, insist that there is no alternative. Economic benefits gained from technology, they maintain, will eventually trickle down to help all Rwandans.

Already these efforts are beginning to yield fruit. In the dusty village of Nyamata, 90 minutes from Kigali, Paul Barera, a 29-year-old Kigali Institute of Science and Technology (KIST) graduate, helps dressmaker Donatille Mukakarara, 38, to use Google to search for new patterns once a week. "The Internet has changed my business," she said. "People want modern designs and that's what I can give them." For Donatille and countless other enterprising Rwandan small-business owners, benefits from the increased use of technology are already evident. For them, the future is quite bright.

CHALLENGES

Environmental degradation and rapid population growth remain critical issues in Rwanda. Before the violence of the 1990s, both conditions clearly threatened the welfare of the general population. On first impression, the recent genocide in

Rwanda appears to be a clear case of environmental and population pressures producing social stress. That stress, in turn, resulted in violent conflict. But on closer study, this is not an adequate explanation of the genocide. Many countries, after all, have experienced severe environmental degradation and high rates of population increase. These conditions did, however, contribute to mass migration, a sharp decline in agricultural productivity, and a weakened presidency, and hence, less effective government.

Governance and Rwanda's Future

Today Rwanda has effective leadership. President Paul Kagame has brought stability to the government. (Kagame's s seven-year term ends in 2010, and he is eligible for a second term in office.) Commenting on him, former president Clinton observed:

> He has gone out of his way to make partnerships . . . to convince all kinds of people just to come in and help Rwanda to build a future. They're not just trying to build an economy: they're trying to build a modern political system and a modern rich culture rooted in who they are without denying where they have been; looking toward where they can go and what they can become. It is a thoroughly astonishing place, well led, but also a place that has lessons to teach us all. Whatever resentments we harbor in our hearts, they pale by the side of what the average Rwandan can carry around and be consumed by every day. They are a lesson in letting go and going on. I hope tonight they'll help us all to learn it well.

CONCLUSION

The tiny, yet strikingly beautiful, country called Rwanda has a very troubled history, but a bright and prosperous future. The number of women in its parliament is unsurpassed by any other country. Harnessing the huge amounts of methane in Lake Kivu and the continued development of biogas promise a lasting solution to the country's current energy crisis. Huge investments in information and communication technology should yield vast dividends for future economic growth. Tourism, based primarily on Rwanda's rare mountain gorillas, has a solid future if only the poachers will stay away. Today the country is beginning to stabilize and prosper under an effective political leadership and government. All Rwanda needs is peace with its neighbors and between its own people. Given sufficient time and peace, Rwanda will become what it was meant to be—*Rwanda Nziza!*—Beautiful Rwanda!

Facts at a Glance

Note: All data 2007 unless otherwise indicated

Physical Geography

Location Central Africa, bordering the Democratic of the Congo, Burundi, Tanzania, and Uganda

Area 10,169 square miles (26,338 square kilometers)

Boundaries Border countries: Burundi, 180 miles (290 kilometers); The Democratic Republic of the Congo, 134.8 miles (217 kilometers); Tanzania, 134.8 miles (217 kilometers), Uganda, 105 miles (169 kilometers)
Total: 893 kilometers

Climate Temperate; two rainy seasons (February to April, November to January); mild in mountains with frost and snow possible

Terrain Mostly grassy uplands and hills; relief is mountainous with altitude declining from west to east

Elevation Extremes Lowest point: Ruzizi River, 3,117 feet (950 meters)
Highest point: Volcan Karisimbi, 14,826 feet (4,519 meters)

Land Use Arable land, 45.56%; permanent crops, 10.25%; other, 44.19% (2005)

Irrigated Land 55.92 square miles (90 square kilometers) (2003)

Natural Hazards Periodic droughts; the volcanic Virunga Mountains are in the northwest along the border with the Democratic Republic of the Congo

Natural Resources Gold, cassiterite (tin ore), wolframite (tungsten ore), methane, hydropower, arable land

Environmental Issues Deforestation results from uncontrolled cutting of trees for fuel; overgrazing; soil exhaustion; soil erosion; widespread poaching

Population & Culture

Population 9,907,509; males, 4,929,459; females, 4,978,050
Note: estimates for this country explicitly take into account the effects of excess mortality due to AIDS; this can result in lower life expectancy, higher infant mortality and death rates, lower population and growth rates, and changes in the distribution of population by age and sex than would otherwise be expected

Population Growth Rate	2.766% (world average: 1.2%)
Net Migration Rate	2.41 migrant(s)/1,000 population
Fertility Rate	5.37 children born/woman
Birthrate	40.16 births/1,000 population
Death Rate	14.91 deaths/1,000 population
Life Expectancy at Birth	Total population: 48.99 years; male, 47.87 years; female, 50.16 years
Median Age	Total: 18.6 years; male, 18.4 years; female, 18.8 years
HIV/AIDS—Adult Prevalence Rate	5.1% (2003 est.)
HIV/AIDS— People Living with HIV/AIDS	250,000 (2003 est.)
HIV/AIDS—Deaths	22,000 (2003 est.)
Ethnic Groups	Hutu (Bantu), 84%; Tutsi (Hamitic), 15%; Twa (Pygmy), 1%
Religion	Roman Catholic, 56.5%; Protestant, 26%; Adventist, 11.1%; Muslim, 4.6%; Indigenous beliefs, 0.1%; none, 1.7% (2001)
Language	Three official languages: Kinyarwanda (universal Bantu vernacular), French, and English; Kiswahili (Swahili) used in commercial centers
Literacy	(Age 15 and over can read and write) Total population: 70.4% (76.3%, male; 64.7%, female)

Economy

Currency	Rwandan franc (RWF)
GDP Purchasing Power Parity (PPP)	$13.7 billion (2006 est.)
GDP Per Capita	$1,600 (2006 est.)
Labor Force	4.6 million (2000)
Unemployment	NA%
Labor Force by Occupation	Agriculture, 90%; industry and services, 10% (2000)
Agricultural Products	Coffee, tea, pyrethrum (insecticide made from chrysanthemums), bananas, beans, sorghum, potatoes; livestock
Industries	Cement, agricultural products, small-scale beverages, soap, furniture, shoes, plastic goods, textiles, cigarettes
Exports	$146 million f.o.b. (2006 est.)
Imports	$436 million f.o.b. (2006 est.)

Leading Trade Partners	Exports: China, 10.3%; Germany, 9.7%; United States, 4.3% (2006); Imports: Kenya, 19.6%; Germany, 7.8%; Uganda, 6.8%; Belgium, 5.1% (2006)
Export Commodities	Coffee, tea, hides, tin ore
Import Commodities	Foodstuffs, machinery and equipment, steel, petroleum products, cement and construction material
Transportation	Roadways: 8,704 miles (14,008 km), 1,654 miles (2,662 km) is paved (2004); Railways: NA; Airports: 9–4 are paved runways; Waterways: Lac Kivu navigable by shallow-draft barges and native craft (2006)
Ports and Terminals	Cyangugu, Gisenyi, Kibuye

Government

Country Name	Conventional long form: Republic of Rwanda; conventional short form: Rwanda; local long form: Republika y'u Rwanda; local short form: Rwanda; former name: Ruanda, German East Africa
Capital City	Kigali
Type of Government	Republic
Chief of State	President Paul Kagame
Independence	July 1, 1962 (from Belgium-administered UN trusteeship)
Administrative Divisions	5 provinces (in French–provinces, singular–province; in Kinyarwanda–prefigintara for singular and plural); East, Kigali, North, South, West
Constitution	New constitution passed by referendum May 26, 2003

Communication

Television Stations	2 (2004)
Radio Stations	AM 0, FM 8
Telephones	312,000 (including 290,000 cell phones) (2005)
Internet Users	65,000 (2006)

1300s Tutsis migrate into what is now Rwanda, which was already inhabited by the Twa and Hutu peoples.

1600s Tutsi king Ruganzu Ndori subdues central Rwanda and outlying Hutu areas.

Late 1800s Tutsi king Kigeri Rwabugiri establishes a unified state with a centralized military structure.

1858 British explorer Hanning Speke is the first European to visit the area.

1890 Rwanda becomes part of German East Africa.

1916 Belgian forces occupy Rwanda.

1923 Belgium granted League of Nations mandate to govern Ruanda-Urundi, which it ruled indirectly through Tutsi kings.

1946 Ruanda-Urundi becomes UN trust territory governed by Belgium.

1957 Hutus issue manifesto calling for a change in Rwanda's power structure to give them a voice commensurate with their numbers; Hutu political parties formed.

1959 Tutsi King Kigeri V, together with tens of thousands of Tutsis, forced into exile in Uganda following interethnic violence.

1961 Rwanda proclaimed a republic.

1962 Rwanda becomes independent with a Hutu, Grègoire Kayibanda, as president; many Tutsis leave the country.

1963 Some 20,000 Tutsis killed following an incursion by Tutsi rebels based in Burundi.

1973 President Grègoire Kayibanda ousted in military coup led by Juvenal Habyarimana.

1978 New constitution ratified; Habyarimana elected president.

1988 Some 50,000 Hutu refugees flee to Rwanda from Burundi following ethnic violence there.

1990 Forces of the rebel Rwandan Patriotic Front (RPF), mainly Tutsi, invade Rwanda from Uganda.

1991	New multiparty constitution promulgated.
1993	President Habyarimana signs a power-sharing agreement with the Tutsis in the Tanzanian town of Arusha, ostensibly signaling the end of civil war; UN mission sent to monitor the peace agreement.
April 1994	Habyarimana and the Burundian president are killed after their plane is shot down over Kigali; the RPF launches a major offensive; extremist Hutu militia and elements of the Rwandan military begin the systematic massacre of Tutsis. Within 100 days, around 800,000 Tutsis and moderate Hutus are killed; Hutu militias flee to Zaire, taking with them around 2 million Hutu refugees.
1994–1996	Refugee camps in Zaire fall under the control of the Hutu militias responsible for the genocide in Rwanda.
1995	Extremist Hutu militias and Zairean government forces attack local Zairean Banyamulenge Tutsis; Zaire attempts to force refugees back into Rwanda.
1995	UN-appointed international tribunal begins charging and sentencing a number of people responsible for the Hutu-Tutsi atrocities.
1996	Rwandan troops invade and attack Hutu militia-dominated camps in Zaire in order to drive home the refugees.
1997	Rwandan- and Ugandan-backed rebels depose President Mobutu Sese Seko of Zaire; Laurent Kabila becomes president of Zaire, which is renamed the Democratic Republic of the Congo.
1998	Rwanda switches allegiance to support rebel forces trying to depose Kabila in the wake of the Congolese president's failure to expel extremist Hutu militias.
March 2000	Rwandan President Pasteur Bizimungu, a Hutu, resigns over differences regarding the composition of a new cabinet and after accusing parliament of targeting Hutu politicians in anti-corruption investigations.

April 2000	Ministers and members of parliament elect Vice President Paul Kagame as Rwanda's new president.
October 2001	Voting to elect members of traditional *gacaca* courts begins. The courts—in which ordinary Rwandans judge their peers—aim to clear the backlog of 1994 genocide cases.
December 2001	A new flag and national anthem are unveiled to try to promote national unity and reconciliation.
April 2002	Former president Pasteur Bizimungu is arrested and faces trial on charges of illegal political activity and threats to state security.
July 2002	Rwanda, DRC sign peace deal under which Rwanda will pull troops out of the DRC and the DRC will help disarm Rwandan Hutu gunmen blamed for killing Tutsi minority in 1994 genocide.
October 2002	Rwanda says it has pulled the last of its troops out of the DRC, four years after they went in to support Congolese rebels against the Kabila government.
May 2003	Voters back a draft constitution that bans the incitement of ethnic hatred.
August 2003	Paul Kagame wins the first presidential elections since the 1994 genocide.
October 2003	First multiparty parliamentary elections; President Kagame's RPF wins absolute majority. EU observers say poll was marred by irregularities and fraud.
December 2003	Three former media directors found guilty of inciting Hutus to kill Tutsis during 1994 genocide and receive lengthy jail sentences.
March 2004	President Kagame rejects French report that says he ordered 1994 attack on president's plane, which sparked genocide.
June 2004	Former president Pasteur Bizimungu is sentenced to 15 years in jail for embezzlement, inciting violence, and associating with criminals.

2005	Main Hutu rebel group FDLR says it is ending its armed struggle. FDLR is one of several groups accused of creating instability in the DRC; many of its members are accused of taking part in 1994 genocide.
July 2005	Government begins the mass release of 36,000 prisoners. Most of them have confessed to involvement in the 1994 genocide. It is the third phase of releases since 2003—part of an attempt to ease overcrowding.
January 2006	Rwanda's 12 provinces are replaced by a smaller number of regions with the aim of creating ethnically diverse administrative areas.
December 2006	Father Athanase Seromba becomes the first Roman Catholic priest to be convicted for involvement in the 1994 genocide. The International Criminal Tribunal sentences him to 15 years in prison.
February 2007	Some 8,000 prisoners accused of genocide are released. Some 60,000 suspects have been freed since 2003 to ease prison overcrowding.
April 2007	Former president Pasteur Bizimungu is released from jail three years into his 15-year sentence after receiving a presidential pardon.

Aryeetey-Attoh, S., eds. *Geography of Sub-Saharan Africa (2nd ed.).* Upper Saddle River, N.J.: Pearson Education, Inc. 2003.

Dallaire, Roméo. *Shake Hands with the Devil: The Failure of Humanity in Rwanda.* New York: Carroll and Graf, 2004.

Gourevitch, Philip. *We Wish to Inform You That Tomorrow We Will Be Killed with Our Families: Stories from Rwanda.* New York: Picador, 1998.

Oppong, J.R. *Africa South of the Sahara.* Philadelphia: Chelsea House Publishers, 2005.

Oppong, J.R. and T. Woodruff. *The Democratic Republic of the Congo.* Philadelphia: Chelsea House Publishers, 2007.

Prunier, Gérard. *The Rwanda Crisis: History of a Genocide.* New York: Columbia University Press, 1995.

Further Reading

Adelman, Howard and Astri Suhrke. *The Path of a Genocide: The Rwanda Crisis from Uganda to Zaire.* Trenton, N.J.: Transaction Books, 1999.

Barnett, Michael N. *Eyewitness to a Genocide: The United Nations and Rwanda.* Ithaca, N.Y.: Cornell University Press, 2002.

Des Forges, Allison. *Leave None to the Tell the Story: Genocide in Rwanda.* New York: Human Rights Watch, 1999.

Hatzfeld, Jean. *Machete Season: The Killers in Rwanda Speak.* New York: Picador, 2006.

Ilibagiza, Immaculée. *Left to Tell: Discovering God Amidst the Rwandan Holocaust.* Carlsbad, C.A.: Hay House, 2006.

Melvern, L.R. *A People Betrayed: The Role of the West in Rwanda's Genocide.* London: Zed Books, 2000.

Rusesabagina, Paul and Tom Zoellner. *An Ordinary Man: An Autobiography.* New York: Viking Press, 2007.

Uvin, Peter. *Aiding Violence: The Development Enterprise in Rwanda.* West Hartford, Conn: Kumarian, 1998.

Web sites

African Studies Center, Rwanda Page
http://www.africa.upenn.edu/Country_Specific/Rwanda.html

Official Web site of the Government of Rwanda
http://www.gov.rw/

Selected Internet resources from Library of Congress on Rwanda
http://www.loc.gov/rr/international/amed/rwanda/rwanda.html

UNDP Rwanda Web site
http://www.unrwanda.org/undp/

Rwanda Tourist Board
http://www.rwandatourism.com/home.htm

Through the Eyes of Children
http://www.rwandaproject.org/

U.S. Department of State, Rwanda page
http://www.state.gov/r/pa/ei/bgn/2861.htm

Human Rights Watch
http://hrw.org/doc/?t=africa&c=rwanda

Global Issues Rwanda
http://www.globalissues.org/Geopolitics/Africa/Rwanda.asp

page:

Index

Index

Index

JOSEPH R. OPPONG is associate professor of geography at the University of North Texas in Denton, Texas, and a native of Ghana. He has nearly two decades of university teaching experience in Ghana, Canada, and the United States. His research focuses on medical geography, the geography of disease and health care. Professor Oppong has authored numerous books for Chelsea House's MODERN WORLD NATIONS series and MAJOR WORLD CULTURES series. He has also served as chairperson of the Association of American Geographers Special Interest Groups on both Africa and medical geography.

CHARLES F. GRITZNER is distinguished professor of geography at South Dakota State University in Brookings. He is now in his fifth decade of college teaching and research. In addition to classroom instruction, he enjoys traveling, writing, working with teachers, and sharing his love of geography with readers. As a senior consulting editor for Chelsea House Publishers' MODERN WORLD NATIONS and MAJOR WORLD CULTURES series, he has a wonderful opportunity to combine each of these "hobbies." Dr. Gritzner has served as both president and executive director of the National Council for Geographic Education and has received the council's highest honor, the George J. Miller Award for Distinguished Service to Geographic Education, as well as other honors from the NCGE, Association of American Geographers, and other organizations.